MW01004474

UNDER PURPLE SKIES

The Minneapolis Anthology

MORE CITY ANTHOLOGIES BY BELT

The Milwaukee Anthology

St. Louis Anthology

The Akron Anthology

Right Here, Right Now: The Buffalo Anthology

Rust Belt Chicago: An Anthology

The Cincinnati Anthology

The Cleveland Anthology

A Detroit Anthology

Happy Anyway: A Flint Anthology

Grand Rapids Grassroots: An Anthology

The Pittsburgh Anthology

Car Bombs to Cookie Tables: The Youngstown Anthology

UNDER PURPLE SKIES
The Minneapolis Anthology

Edited by Frank Bures

Copyright © 2019, Belt Publishing
All rights reserved. This book or any portion thereof may not be reproduced or used in any
manner whatsoever without the express written permission of the publisher except for the use
of brief quotations in a book review.

First Edition 2019
ISBN: 978-1948742436

Belt Publishing
3143 W. 33rd Street, Cleveland, Ohio 44109
www.beltpublishing.com

Book design by Meredith Pangrace
Cover by David Wilson

contents

contents

contents

Prologue

FRANK BURES

The entire area of Minneapolis, before a storm, the skies would turn this amazing blue-purple before the rain came. It was a phenomenon. So for me, the concept of "purple rain" was very specific in terms of the feeling you get just before the clouds would open up and literally gush raindrops. Later on, when Prince and I were working at Paisley Park, we would go outside prior to a rainstorm and just stand in the field, looking at the sky together. Waiting for the rain to drop. And those skies went purple.

—Albert Magnoli, *Director, editor, and co-writer of* Purple Rain, *in* GQ

Years ago, when I left Minneapolis I brought a book with me: *Coming Home Crazy: An Alphabet of China Essays*. It was published by a local publisher, Milkweed Editions, and written by a Minnesota author, performer, and force of nature, Bill Holm, about his year teaching English in China in the late 1980s.

Holm was an unforgettable figure—cantankerous, joyful, angry, and full of laughter. He was also emblematic of the Minnesota writers in those days, coming (as he and I both did) from a line of northern European immigrant farmers.

Reading Holm was a revelation. He broke the mold of what an essay could do, and I was inspired by all the things on display in his work: his ability to laugh at absurdity, his attempts at understanding, his distrust of authority, his populism seeping into every sentence. I didn't know you could do all that—or how you did it.

In particular there was an essay I loved called "Swiss Army Knife: A History" about the many times Holm used his knife in China to fix sparking lamps, open cans of dog meat, disconnect propaganda speakers, and take doors off their hinges.

As I attempted to find my way as a writer, I would occasionally reread this essay and try to emulate Holm's style and voice. But I didn't have the depth of experience to turn life into art. Today I still can't write like Holm, but I did manage to find my own path. And when I went to China to research my own book, I brought a copy of his essay and my Swiss Army Knife, only to find that China had changed, as had I. The world Holm described was long gone, replaced by a new, stranger, wealthier China where things (mostly) worked. All I needed the knife for was opening an occasional beer.

When I moved back to Minneapolis I found the city had changed as well. It was more international. The food was better. There were more bikes and fewer murders. The once plucky local publishers had become national literary treasures. And the writers at work here weren't so much from the same lineages of Scandinavians who came here to farm and enjoyed making each other feel guilty.

Like me, the city had picked up stories from other parts of the world—Somalia, Laos, Mexico, Vietnam, Nigeria, Jamaica, and others, not to mention White Earth, Leech Lake, and the state's other Anishinaabe and Dakota communities. I found these stories as compelling as anything that had happened in Gopher Prairie or Lake Wobegon. Not only did the city's narrative threads now run from different corners of the world, but whenever the national (and sometimes international) literary prizes were announced, there was almost certain to be a writer or publisher from around here among the ranks. While I was away, the Twin Cities had somehow become a literary powerhouse.

With that in mind, we have collected a sampling of some of the best work being done in or about this city that casts its long shadow across the state. Most of writers in *Under Purple Skies* live in Minneapolis or the larger Twin Cities. Others here have passed through and told great stories about it. Still others live farther away, like Luisa Muradyan. Growing up in the Soviet Union (now Ukraine), she watched a bootleg copy of *Purple Rain*. "My family was so transfixed with the movie," she writes, "that they thought it was set in the future. The music, the clothing, the magnificence, this movie became the narrative of America that my family would later pursue through immigration. Prince touched so many lives, including a Soviet family that would later turn to his music as a soundtrack for assimilation."

Of course, Prince is the specter that hangs over the city, and this collection. He's the one who showed us that you can create your own world right here, rather than chasing after it elsewhere. And just as the purple sky he loved meant change was in the air, so does this collection show the literary storm that is washing over us.

Collectively, the writers here have won, or been shortlisted for, the Newbery Award, the Man Booker prize, the Pulitzer, the Caldecott Award, the National Book Award, the Minnesota Book Award, and many others. Their work appears alongside new and first-time voices. But Minnesotans don't like to brag, and prizes are beside the point. The stories and poems here should speak for themselves. And in the same way Holm's generation showed mine a path, I hope this collection paves the way for the writers who will follow.

Introduction

LAURIE HERTZEL

In the summer of 1966, my father put on a literature workshop about north country writers at the university where he taught English. He brought in J. F. Powers, who had recently won a National Book Award for *Morte d'Urban*; Robert Bly, who was just about to win a National Book Award for *The Light Around the Body*; and Sigurd Olson, who lived up in Ely and wrote about paddling through the wilderness. He also assigned the students to read the works of August Derleth, Hamlin Garland, Glenway Wescott and—Yes! A woman!—Zona Gale.

These were all solid midwestern writers. They were quite different from one another. Bly wrote poetry. Olson wrote homey essays on the wilderness. Powers wrote novels. But they also had much in common. Their roots were in the prairie and the woods. They were proudly provincial, living and writing within the borders they knew.

In the years since my father's workshop, those borders have expanded dramatically. At the same time, Minneapolis has quietly, steadily, and rather stupendously grown into one of the most sophisticated literary centers in the country. It is well known for its excellent small presses, its fine poets, writers and spoken-word artists, its wealth of independent bookstores and esteemed MFA programs, and, yes, its diversity.

I have been the books editor at the *Minneapolis Star Tribune* for a decade, and during those years I've done my best to keep track of Minnesota writers old and new—their books, their awards, their appearances, their rise. But keeping track is a stunning, careening cartwheel of a job, reading the gritty poetry of Danez Smith and the big-hearted novels of Charles Baxter and the magical, weird short stories of Lesley Nneka Arimah, the poignant, lovely essays of Kao Kalia Yang, the mysteries of Ellen Hart, the novels of National Book Award-winner Louise Erdrich, the poems of her sister Heid, and the outlandish, violent, fascinating novels of Man Booker Prize-winner Marlon James.

And often, so very, very often, a book crosses my desk by yet another Minnesota writer that I haven't yet heard of. Mystery writers, poets—oh, we are gorgeous with poets—essayists, novelists, scholars, historians, and biographers. We are wonderfully awash in writers—emerging, fledgling, established, venerable.

Back in my father's day, we had the idea that all notable Minnesota writers were of a certain type: Sinclair Lewis, F. Scott Fitzgerald, Jon Hassler, Tim O'Brien, Frederick Manfred, Bill Holm. That is, white, male, and straight. Today that spotlight is widening and making room. In 2012, when half of the winners of the National Book Awards were from Minnesota, one was a Native American writer (Louise Erdrich) and the other a Cuban-American writer (Will Alexander).

A confluence of events in the 1970s and 1980s started this movement just a few years after my father held that workshop. Scott Walker moved Graywolf Press from Washington state to St. Paul (it is now in Minneapolis); Allan Kornblum moved Coffee House Press up to Minneapolis from Iowa; Bill Truesdale brought New Rivers Press to the Twin Cities from out East (the press is now in Moorhead); Emilie Buchwald and R. W. Scholes started a journal called the *Milkweed Chronicle*, which turned into the publisher Milkweed Editions; and Marly Rusoff started the Loft Literary Center in a loft above a bookstore in Dinkytown. (The Loft's first reading—an impromptu affair—was by Robert Bly.)

For many years, there was a steady flow of grant and fellowship money that helped keep writers afloat. (That flow continues, though it is less robust.) The Loft and the small presses formed a supportive community that has continued to grow and produce other organizations, some long-lived, some short-lived, some now defunct but all making a difference for writers—SASE, a Place for Writers; Intermedia Arts; the Minneapolis Writers Workshop (which predates them all); and a million book clubs and writers series.

And it must be said that the weather—frigid and confining as it is for months at a time—helps. "People elsewhere think that it's cold and desolate around these parts, but that cold is good for literacy and reading and culture," Louise Erdrich once said in a *Star Tribune* interview. "We live in a very special place, and I'm glad to call it home."

This anthology of new writing by Minneapolis writers represents some of the finest writers anywhere. Some were born here. Others, to our great good fortune, moved here. A few have moved away. But all have been touched, in some way, by the city, and their literary strands are now woven into the fabric of this place.

These new writers cross all borders—young, old; white, of color; straight, gay. Like their predecessors, some of them are grounded by the land, but that is only one of their tethers. As Danez Smith writes in the poem "I'm Going Back to Minnesota Where Sadness Makes Sense,"

I'm bored with the ocean
I stood at the lip of it, dressed in down, praying for snow

But Smith draws on so much more than geography for his inspiration. He draws on race, and love, and being HIV positive. Matt Rasmussen is inspired by place too. He writes about the demolished Metrodome:

From afar you looked like someone
strapped down a cloud

or built a giant pillow
for the sky. But why?

Elsewhere he writes of sorrow and loss and family and suicide.

Back in 1966, my father's seminar grappled with the question of what defines northern writers. The weather? The Scandinavian stoicism? In the end, they came to no conclusion.

"I think the whole subject deserves more attention," my father wrote in a piece for *South Dakota Review* that summed up the conference. "Regardless of all the talk about Southern writers and the grainy complexity of the Southern stand, there are some interesting things going on in the North."

This is more true now than ever.

Little House with the Shared Wall

KAO KALIA YANG

When you bought the house you did not think of me. You thought instead of the alley where you parked your car, the backs of the fine houses that looked out on Milwaukee Avenue, the only street in the city where cars are banned and you must pass on foot. Two blocks of storybook brick and wood houses, a bubble of history from the 1880s, with high porches and cushioned seats, flower baskets hanging low, gardens full of dahlias in bloom, roses climbing trellises, flowers in accordance with the seasons. You thought of the Ace Hardware two doors down, the bar around the corner, the popular pizza place across the avenue, the little string of lights that illuminated the windows of the bustling coffee shop, the high-end hair salon upstairs, the book shop at the end of the block, the co-op of organic foods a few blocks down. In a landscape with so few Hmong people present, how could you have ever envisioned that you'd end up with one?

You told me that it had once belonged to a professor at the university, an old bachelor who had died. You liked gray, so the inside was wood and metal, accented by the touches of your then-girlfriend, a designer who liked to make sweater clothing for rocks, tree branches, and other objects she found in the natural world. She, who I've never met except in pictures, must have liked to keep things warm—even when they are meant to be cold.

The front of the house was divided in two: a few steps on each side led to low porches side-by-side, on each porch there was a door, and each door led into the separate halves of the house. You lived on the right. An older couple lived on the left. On the right of your house was an open yard, a stretch of tended, spotted lawn that the dogs in the neighborhood enjoyed peeing and pooping in. To the left of your neighbor's side, there was a wild garden, full of dogwood bushes, knee-high grass, clusters of thriving chives, the spread of mint, and other flowering plants.

When I met you, you'd been in the house for four of your thirty-one years. I was twenty-nine. I had no idea that such a place existed in Minnesota, where I'd lived since I was six years old. I had no idea that there was a "walking avenue" in Minneapolis. No knowledge of the people who lived along its lane, houses with paintings on walls, shelves full of books, windows that faced each other, backed into other houses, protected from the streets I knew and traveled on. When I saw the world from your bedroom window, I saw how on misty evenings, the lights of the city glowed like a film across the dark expanse of night.

When we got married and I moved into that house with you, I brought little with me because I had little to bring. I'd come from a community full of people, a family full of generations, a life full of love, but filled with little by way of things. I knew the call of the drums of the dead, the cry of the morning roosters when pink unfolded across the dawn sky, the sway of the prairie grass in lonely tandem with the plaintive tones from the Hmong *qeej*. Educated in America, building a life here, I had not thought of what my marriage or my love would look and feel like across the distance between you, a white man safe in his privilege and powers, and me, a first-generation Hmong refugee woman.

In the beginning, like many love stories, that little house with the shared walls was full of wonder and magic. I remember how we kept the bedroom windows opened as often as we could, during early spring, throughout hot summer, late into the fall and early winter months. We slept on different pillows, our hands held tight, listening to the fights from the men and women in the apartment buildings across the street. One particularly loud spring night, a man yelled, "I have been waiting all winter to argue with you, Woman!" and I remembered how life had been when I was a child, all eight of us in a 900-square-foot house on the east side of St. Paul, how we trailed our mother and father from one room to the next, colliding in small hallways, putting hands to heads and holding our breaths deep inside so we took up less space. Another night, two drunken men, walking slowly shoulder to shoulder, leaning heavily on one another mumbled their love, "We love, love, love each other, you and I." They took turns saying these words, again and again. In that gray bedroom, beside the framed Afghan rug, in the dark of our room, there on that bed beneath the moonlight, you and I recited their words to each other again and again like a meditation, like a prayer, like breath.

Before we learned how to have satisfying, productive fights, we yelled and screamed our anger and frustration—heedless of the shared wall in between us and Sarah and Myron, the elderly musicians on the other side. Our inner yards were flipped: we were the ones with grass growing high, flowering bushes and weeds, mint growing unheeded. They were the lawn, tended, spotted, but well-loved.

We were loud, full of quick breaths and quick words, our emotions like bullets from our smoking guns. I grabbed the keys to the single car we shared and stormed from one door to the other, looking for a way out. My big green jacket falling off my shoulders in the heat of frustration. You raced me to one door and then the other, preventing easy escape. One time, you were so angry at me, you pushed so hard within yourself, your eyes bulged, and the pores on your face turned red, the blood unleashed from pressure within. I remember laughing inside and out at the ridiculous temper you had, your inability to control your anger when my own was a cyclone blowing me wild. I remember how hurt you were at my laughter. How could I be so immature at twenty-nine? How could you be so stupid as to propose to a woman two months after meeting her? We did not know what it took, what it would take, to make a marriage work, let alone the one we had, two people in a colonized world, a world where white men like you killed men and women of color like me with far too much regularity and far too little consequence. Our little home exploded with the issues of a bigger world, its walls weak.

There was no place to put our frustrations on Milwaukee Avenue. There was no room for the disruption to the flowers in bloom, to the empty porches with cushioned seats, the windows that opened up to houses full of music and literature, full of art and the safety of a white world. Because there were no spaces around us, we, like the man and the woman on the other side of the street, once the snow had melted and spring had sprung, took our frustrations where we could; we filled that little house with the shared wall with our hopes and our dreams, the sorrow and the despair, the desperation of our love.

We lived in that little house together for four years. By the time we moved out, we had gotten pregnant and lost the baby, a boy who looked like me. His body was soft and sagging. His mouth was opened like a hungry bird's. His eyes were closed but the skin on top of them was so light I could almost see through them to what I imagined was a small universe of possibility, dark and dead.

By the time we moved out, we had gotten pregnant again and in our arms, we carried a little girl, nearly two years old, who looked like both of us. She had your eyebrows, straight and fine. She had my small nose. She did not sleep much; we did not sleep much. Her eyes, pearls of gray and green, looked upon the world with the light of life, shining bright and unafraid. When we left that little house, my belly was swollen with the bodies of two little boys, floating in a shared world, twisting and turning, looking already for a way to live in our love story, fraught with danger.

When we left the house, we left the floors shiny, we left the lights on all over the house, we left the gray walls bare for the man and woman who had found the house together, who had seen in it possibilities for the both of them to grow, for their love story to blossom and bloom close to Milwaukee Avenue.

Now, years later, I think back to that house, to the many nights we looked out its windows, not at the lights of the city across the rooftops, but at the full moon in the dark sky, its face full of scars.

Counting Swallows

MORGAN GRAYCE WILLOW

Flight patterns
above this intersection
where two cities meet,
announce that mosquitoes
have hatched this mid-May day.
There might be three,
or maybe a dozen swallows,
crossing the window frame
though never all at once,
and never simply left to right.
Instead their ellipses flatten,
loop, elongate into infinity signs,
a calligraphy of hunger
against pale blue.

The City by Segway

DOUG MACK

One day, I decided to become a Segway tour guide on the Minneapolis riverfront. I needed the money. I needed the fresh air. I needed to get out of my comfort zone. And showing complete strangers around my beloved city from the perch of our era's most ridiculed mode of transportation checked all the boxes.

At the time I was thirty years old and single. The view from my blue microfiber futon overlooked a weedy parking lot. But from the front door of my apartment building, it was a straight four-block shot to the Mississippi riverfront, a whole new world of lushness and cobblestones, where the nation's most storied waterway, wide and muddy, eased past the limestone mills that built the city, and which were now in various states of ruin and revival. Here was Main Street, every bit the Norman Rockwell scene conjured by its name, with historic brick buildings, cozy cafés, and families out for a stroll (parents holding hands, kids on scooters, a beagle bounding alongside them), and in the middle of it all, the incongruous scene of rookie Segway riders lurching atop their self-balancing steeds, yelping and flailing and trying their damnedest not fall on their faces.

I wanted to be part of that tableau. All of it. And though the family part wasn't anywhere on the horizon given the dismal state of my dating life (so many awkward conversations, so few connections), the Segway part was just a job interview away.

Before long I got hired and outfitted: yellow t-shirt, red helmet, walkie-talkie. I learned to run the cash register and to answer the most common questions: *How fast can these things go?* About twelve miles per hour, max. *How much do they cost?* Around five grand. *Is it true that the inventor of the Segway died while he was riding one?* Not true! But the guy who bought the company and served as its CEO . . . yeah. He drove his Segway off a cliff by accident. That won't happen to you, most likely!

A Segway is a technological marvel, self-balancing thanks to five gyroscopes and a solid-state angular rate sensor. (Say this with a straight face and move on before anyone asks for further explanation.) It's all hidden inside the base upon which you stand. What you actually see, what registers in your mind, is a pogo stick affixed to a small plastic box with two wheels attached, a prank cobbled together with stuff found in the garage. Your lizard brain pulses a warning: *You're going to fall on your face.*

The key is to block out that voice, to turn off your brain. It's all about subtle movements and adjustments, like downhill skiing, only slower and more nerdy: lean a bit on your toes to go forward, shift to your heels to slow down. For every human action, there's a mechanical reaction—if you fight it, it'll fight back. Be cool, find your balance. As our tours began, riders would still be working on this, forming a weaving line of a dozen or more Segways, an absurdist Make Way for Ducklings, with yellow-shirted guides nudging their charges along, reminding them not to overthink it.

The tour featured seven history stops, and most guides maintained the keep-it-simple approach in their spiels. They weren't historians, they were a random assortment of summer-job-seekers: college students and artists and aspiring entrepreneurs; a retired principal and a kindergarten teacher who always tried to work her favorite bar—"Home of the Greenie!"—into her talks. Where entertainment is the point and tips are on the line, a good story takes precedence over verifiable fact. Hit the highlights, bullshit at will.

Our first stop was in front of the Pillsbury A-Mill, a mass of grey limestone, the world's largest flour mill when it opened in 1881. It was here, on my first tour, that I heard the first whopper, a claim that, because the building was listed on the National Register of Historic Places, nothing on the interior or exterior could be altered or removed, including machinery. If the planned conversion to apartments ever happened, the guide said with utmost sincerity, people would have to put beds on top of grinders and build bathrooms around sifters.

This is not true. I knew it was not true because it is obviously not true, but also because my father is a historic preservation architect and I knew how these things work—all of which I desperately wanted to yell out on that first tour. But more than anything, I wanted to fit in, to be part of the team of guides, and to get those tips and maybe, eventually, upgrade that blue microfiber futon or even get out of that apartment. Be cool, I reminded myself. Find your balance.

I quickly realized that the talking points varied not just from guide to guide but from day to day. Tales of the riverfront came and went, intersected with the truth, then veered away. It was history edited on the fly, depending on weather, mood, crowd size, and the need to get to the bathroom. I started gently offering suggestions when facts got truly mangled over and over, trying my best not to be pedantic. But after I began doing history stops myself, I discovered the ease with which the truth got jumbled, due to nerves or the sudden desire for a quick hit of laughter from my audience, not unlike the bumbling small-talk on the first dates that filled many of my evenings that summer.

From the mill, a path led us through shady Father Hennepin Park—named for a Franciscan missionary who came here in 1680—and then to the Stone Arch Bridge and the view of the skyline and Saint Anthony Falls—*Owámniyomni,* to use the Dakota name that was in our official script but which we were too embarrassed to attempt to pronounce. At the falls, we were supposed to talk about how back when Father Hennepin was here and it hadn't eroded so much, it was much higher . . . and at this point, my brain always froze. *How high was it?* Some guides said it was as tall as Niagara, some said it was forty feet high, another said one hundred feet. No matter how many times I looked it up, I always forgot, so I'd quickly point at the Guthrie Theater—a decidedly modern building with dark-blue cladding and hulking mass offset by a golden glass box near the top—and deadpan that it was the North American headquarters for Ikea. If they laughed, I'd say the whole thing came flat-pack, and was put together with a single Allen wrench. Keep riffing, keep 'em happy, get those tips.

But no wisecracks or facts—fumbled or not—could compete with the setting. That magnificent horseshoe-shaped waterfall, those shimmering skyscrapers just blocks from the river. Minneapolis combined the urban and the pastoral like nowhere else I knew, and for all my apprehensions about what I was doing, there was an undeniable pleasure in sharing this place with other people. For a few minutes, we were immersed together in the heart of the city, its defining tragedies and triumphs written in the stones and trees and waterway around us.

On weekend afternoons, wedding parties took over the area around the Stone Arch Bridge for photo shoots, and we'd veer around them, bridesmaids and groomsmen giving us thumbs-up and high-fives or, sometimes, just pointing and laughing. All we could do was mug and bask, knowing that our weird scooters had just added a jolt of absurdity to a solemn occasion, mingling sacred and profane.

As the summer wore on, I became more confident in my history talks, finding a balance of straight facts and crowd-pleasing humor, and also more secure as part of the team, bantering with the other guides, trusting them. But when I saw all those happy-family tableaus on Main Street or on the Stone Arch Bridge, there was always a sense of something missing, a story still jumbled and incomplete: I wanted my own quiet riverfront moment with someone I loved.

I kept going on dates, and at the beginning of August, I met Maren, a graduate student with brown hair and a constant gleam in her blue-green eyes. It took me a couple of dates to work up to mentioning my nascent career as a Segway tour guide, but finally I blurted it out with a combination of pride and sheepishness. One week later, we walked the route together on a quiet Sunday morning with a choir of cicadas singing the hymns. Everything felt right: the company, the conversation, the setting.

The topics meandered, finally getting deeper than the getting-to-know-you chitchat of our earlier dates, and pausing now and then for Maren to prompt me, with a gentle smirk, for some history. As we passed the downtown post office, I told her about its brass light fixture, three hundred feet long or something like that, but *really freaking long, it's so cool.* We kept going across the Hennepin Avenue Bridge—*Those suspension cables? Just for show, not structurally necessary*—and up to the village on Nicollet Island. A place where even the Twin Cities locals did wonderstruck double-takes at the two dozen historic houses—a Queen Anne here, a Colonial there—under a canopy of oaks and elms, movie-set idyllic. "I've lived in Minneapolis for forty years and I had no idea this was here," one woman told me. One day, a family of foxes trotted by as we rode down the island's brick streets. Maren, too, hadn't known about the village, and it was all I could do to suppress giddiness as I pointed out the shortcut paths winding through the woods, the purple house and the yellow one, and the micro-prairie where, in late-summer evenings, the tall grasses glowed.

In the coming months, we would walk around this area many times, as a couple. The next year, I would move into her apartment on the other side of the city; a year after that, we would get married. Maren's bachelorette party would include a Segway tour led by the kindergarten teacher with a fondness for the Greenie.

But on that first riverfront walk, we took a detour from the Segway route, to a landing along the riverbank, hidden from the main road on Nicollet Island. It was my favorite spot in the city, a place I sometimes came to sit quietly, a place where history and nature seemed to wrap around me like a blanket, cozy and calming. All of downtown was laid out before us, towering and magnificent, just across the water. I had no talking points, no history, no jokes. We sat in silence, enjoying the city together, fully belonging in this place together.

Distortion

TODD BOSS

for Wilbur B. Foshay

Every floor
of your Tower
is by square feet
smaller
than the one
just one floor
below. As you're
lifted
from the street
to the penthouse
suite, you can't
see the walls
draw inward,
but they do.
The windows, too:
Each neat row
frames a richer,
more complete,
and yet some-
how a flatter
view that
angles nearer
the higher you go.
The elevator
bell (though
who could ever
tell?) grows
ever so
faintly clearer.

One would never
call it what it is:
a distortion.

And the rider
grows larger
by proportion.

Wilbur B. Foshay was an American businessman who made a fortune in utilities and built the Foshay Tower in Minneapolis, a twenty-three-story art deco skyscraper sloped like the Washington Monument. In 1932 he was convicted of conducting a pyramid scheme with shares of his own stock. Foshay's trial was a public spectacle with Foshay claiming colorblindness to explain peculiar marks in his accounting books—"in the red" and "in the black" were marked by symbols rather than ink color—when really these marks represented which entries were artificially inflated. He was sentenced to fifteen years in prison.

Sewers

BILL DONAHUE

It is a splendid sound, the clattering of a manhole cover thrown against asphalt. First there is a high, scratchy *clank*, and then, as the lid wobbles on the hard ground, a low, gravely roar, a couple of pings, and finally a quiet thud that gives way, this time, to silence. Peter Sand utters not a word. The bony, young maestro of the Minneapolis sewer system is merely straddling the denuded manhole and savoring the Stygian sights. Beneath him is a gray pipe that offers just four rusted ladder rungs before it drops ten feet to a shoe-box-narrow ledge above a brisk night-black underground river, depth unknown, but probably increasing, thanks to this evening's thunderstorms.

"It looks dangerous," Sand murmurs with a faint relish. "Let's go." As two acolytes spot him, Sand casts a homemade ladder—a rope-and-dowels contraption he built this afternoon—into the pit and then clambers downward, a fey kid in baggy skate shorts and plastic sandals surrendering his fate to his own jury-rigged gear.

"This ladder is, uh, very flexible," he shouts up to the surface. "It bends as much as a foot each time you step on it." He keeps going, and then, near the bottom, his slender legs swing out and he comes to rest on the ledge.

A straight-A computer science major at Carnegie Mellon University, Sand looks a bit like Robert Oppenheimer, the bombmaker, standing there. In four years of lurking beneath his hometown, he has become intimate with its gritty, century-old labyrinth of tunnels—with their rats; their ghostly, slow-swimming carp; their two-inch-long cockroaches; their gushes of clear storm water; their beautiful waterfalls; and their pungent bounties of human waste. He is shooting a ten-minute film—a nightmarish piece about a man being chased in the tunnels, and has displayed a hacker's ingenuity for creating cheap sewering gear—a boat made out of an old file cabinet, for instance. ("Why use a $2,000 canoe," he muses, "when it could get sucked away down a tunnel shaft?") He has straddled the perilously thin gap between bravery and stupidity. Once he climbed an eighty-foot, algae-slimed ladder in darkness at 2:00 a.m., without safety ropes.

Tonight, Sand aims to reach the finest of all underground waterfalls—a roaring twenty-five-foot cascade that is the crown jewel of subterranean Bassett Creek. He waits for his cronies to bungle their way down to the ledge, and then he knots a scrap of rope around his waist and has them dangle him down to the water. He stands; the current does not bowl him over. "It's fine," he says. Then, deep in the earth, the trio slogs east toward the waterfall. They trudge on for fifteen minutes, until the stream underfoot becomes ominously, unmanageably deep. On an earlier trip, someone spied a clump of sewer-borne pantyhose dangling from a head-high hook on a tunnel wall—evidence of how fully the tunnels can flood, how real the threat of inundation can be. They scurry west, out of the pipes.

All cities are endowed with the municipal equivalent of a subconscious. Paris is underlain with six layers of chalk catacombs, New York is home to a seven-level secret city that is home to as many as 5,000 "mole people." The richness of sub-sidewalk Minneapolis lies in its sandstone. The city is built over the St. Peter Sandstone, a vast stratum that sprawls throughout the Midwest, and it sits above a portion particularly close to the surface, which means that Minneapolis is riddled with caves—and that the city's fathers had to cut only fifty feet below ground to attain a wide band of rock that yields to pickaxes yet doesn't collapse.

The fifty-four miles of tunnels beneath are carved into the sandstone. They are, in bureaucrats' terms, an attractive nuisance. The subterranean system of neighboring St. Paul had seen several tragedies—a man was killed and another paralyzed in 1984, and two teenaged girls died of carbon-monoxide poisoning in 1992. Jodi Polzin, an engineer with the Minneapolis Department of Public Works, is bracing for the worst. "What happens if a storm breaks out when those kids are down there?" she asks. "They'd have no escape. What happens if someone's dumped an illegal toxin in the waters they're wading through? It'd take a very long time for a rescue team to show up." Sewering is a misdemeanor in Minnesota, and the stinking tunnels could harbor criminals. All of which, perversely, seems merely to ramp up the appeal of the underground for a certain sort of foolhardy young thrill-seeker. Peter Sand's brand of because-it's-there exploration doesn't set out for the top of the world; it slips into the fetid sewers—without helmets or headlamps.

When he was eighteen, Sand learned of Minneapolis's largest sandstone cavern, the Farmers and Mechanics Bank Cave. A city-block-size-system underneath downtown, the cave has been infamous ever since the City Sewer Department warned, in a 1929 public announcement, that it might collapse, causing unparalleled calamity. It appears on the city's sewer-system maps, and when Sand noticed it, it sang to him as a "dark underworld right beneath the happy glass skyscrapers." In an uncharacteristic burst of effusion, he christened the cavern "The Holy Grail." Then he began searching for it.

By the time we get downtown, a cop is cruising the area and wondering what Sand's mostly teenage coterie of seven is doing on the streets at midnight. "Do you know where you are?" asks the officer.

"Yes," replies Matt, a physics major at the University of Minnesota.

"Do you know where you're going?"

"Yes," he repeats. The officer motors away.

"Very existential," Matt opines, his silver eyebrows dancing over his spectacles. Laughter titters through the ranks, and then we plunge underground—twenty feet down a built-in ladder, into a cathedral-shaped room three feet deep in backwash from the cold Mississippi. Beyond, in the shadowy glimmer of our flashlights, is an oblong pipe fourteen-feet-high and wrought of ancient bricks and limestone. We follow it in, our feet sloshing in the echoing tube.

After a while, we crawl through a trapdoor and encounter a putrid, organic stench: a sanitary sewer. The water below is brown, and thundering in its speed. We stand there for a moment, registering its grossness. Then one tunneler sidles up to a girl in the group and, in earnest tones, confides, "That's human waste. Don't breathe. Methane is toxic."

The girl says nothing, and winces.

Sand, in contrast, seems hopeful. The torrent, which he has christened "The Raging River," leads, he says, directly to the grail. He and Matt once waded up it in shorts for a full third of a mile, risking cholera (not to mention a lifetime of ill-fortune on the dating circuit). Matt slipped; he went under, glasses and all. He got his footing, finally, by jamming his knees into the culvert's seamed floor.

"Matt didn't get sick," Sand says as he stands by the churning brown water, "so the only real danger here is the sewage-processing turbines downstream. All we need to do is stretch a cargo net across the river to prevent people from being washed away to the treatment facility."

The next morning, after taking a thorough shower, Sand picks up Matt and me and drives the minivan into St. Paul to have breakfast with a sewering colleague that Sand had previously encountered only online—geologist Greg Brick. If Sand is sewering's crafty young innovator, Brick is the subculture's wizened elder. Indeed, he calls himself "The Philosopher of the Sewers." In his years of exploration, he has published more than a dozen papers on the subterranean city. He has swum through a tunnel that undercuts Salt Lake's Mormon Tabernacle and lived to tell the tale of a forty-foot underground ladder that crumbled in his hand "like a Dutch pretzel."

Sand sits quietly, nibbling his toast. When he speaks, it's to seek Brick's insights on routes to the grail. Sand seems to regard the entire sewer system schematically, as a sort of a mathematical proof begging solutions. And he recounts an expedition in which his calculations proved almost fatal. Pursuing the grail, he had guided a damaged, rock-filled canoe into a flooded pipe. The water rose until just two inches of air space remained. "My cousin was tied to the canoe," Sand says. "He was underwater, trying to cut the rope with his knife." Sand smiled, dismissing the memory. "But in the end, he was fine. He cut himself free."

After the bill comes, I stepped outside with Brick. "Those guys aren't just reckless," he said. "They're oblivious to how dangerous the sewers can be."

As it turns out, Brick has his own dreams of penetrating the Farmers and Mechanics Bank Cave, and somewhat grudgingly, on a hot Sunday in August, he collaborates with Sand to push for the grail. Brick stands on the street in a fluorescent orange vest, lifting manhole lids. Meanwhile, Sand descends the long, dark shafts, probing for routes to the cave. At one point, he spends forty-five minutes trudging through an uncharted stream of sewage. "I thought I was going to have to tell his mother he'd died," Brick says.

But Sand emerges with news: the stream slices sharply downward, into the Raging River and, quite probably, toward the cave.

The next night, Brick begs off on account of fatigue; Sand returns with Matt and another friend, Tom. Sand carries a homemade wooden ladder built expressly for entering the cave, but the roiling tributary sucks it away and tosses Sand off balance. He stands sideways, surf-sliding on the slippery floor, but it's useless: the stream knocks him on his butt. He loses his flashlight, and in the pitch blackness he slams against something hard: the ladder.

Sand loses a patch of skin on his hand and is so bruised that his body will ache for weeks. Tom swallows something nasty; he'll later contract giardiasis. Nevertheless, Peter Sand's fifty-first—and, he swears, final—foray into the Minneapolis underworld presses on.

Just off the Raging River is a ladder so rusted and brittle that it crumbles when touched. Sand jams his own ladder into its shaft and climbs up. The holes he finds above him are just big enough: sand and his minions make it into the grail.

"It wasn't as vast as I thought it would be," Sand will say later. "It was basically a series of small eight-foot-high chambers separated by columns of concrete and sandstone. It was like a maze, with piles of sewage and little gray bugs shaped like armadillos. But it was, uh . . . interesting. There were these turn-of-the-century brick downspouts that sent water into clear pools. It felt like we were archaeologists entering a pyramid built by people long dead."

They stayed for twenty minutes, then struggled downstream, climbing out past the "death holes," a series of human-size slits in the channel that hurtle waste toward the treatment facility. "We hiked out through a long, almost-dry tunnel," Sand eventually tells me "and then swam out into the Mississippi. It felt good to be in the clean water."

The Minneapolis Poem

JAMES WRIGHT

to John Logan

1

I wonder how many old men last winter
Hungry and frightened by namelessness prowled
The Mississippi shore
Lashed blind by the wind, dreaming
Of suicide in the river.
The police remove their cadavers by daybreak
And turn them in somewhere.
Where?
How does the city keep lists of its fathers
Who have no names?
By Nicollet Island I gaze down at the dark water
So beautifully slow.
And I wish my brothers good luck
And a warm grave.

2

The Chippewa young men
Stab one another shrieking
Jesus Christ.
Split-lipped homosexuals limp in terror of assault.
High school backfields search under benches
Near the Post Office.
Their faces are the rich
Raw bacon without eyes.
The Walker Art Center crowd stare
At the Guthrie Theater.

3

Tall Negro girls from Chicago
Listen to light songs.

They know when the supposed patron
Is a plainclothesman.
A cop's palm
Is a roach dangling down the scorched fangs
Of a light bulb.
The soul of a cop's eyes
Is an eternity of Sunday daybreak in the suburbs
Of Juárez, Mexico.

4

The legless beggars are gone, carried away
By white birds.
The Artificial Limbs Exchange is gutted
And sown with lime.
The whalebone crutches and hand-me-down trusses
Huddle together dreaming in a desolation
Of dry groins.
I think of poor men astonished to waken
Exposed in broad daylight by the blade
Of a strange plough.

5

All over the walls of comb cells
Automobiles perfumed and blindered
Consent with a mutter of high good humor
To take their two naps a day.
Without sound windows glide back
Into dusk.
The sockets of a thousand blind bee graves tier upon tier
Tower not quite toppling.
There are men in this city who labor dawn after dawn
To sell me my death.

6

But I could not bear
To allow my poor brother my body to die
In Minneapolis.
The old man Walt Whitman our countryman
Is now in America our country

Dead.
But he was not buried in Minneapolis
At least.
And no more may I be
Please God.

7

I want to be lifted up
By some great white bird unknown to the police,
And soar for a thousand miles and be carefully hidden
Modest and golden as one last corn grain,
Stored with the secrets of the wheat and the mysterious lives
Of the unnamed poor.

The Minneapolis Poem

DOBBY GIBSON

When I see an airplane pass overhead
I sometimes imagine there are celebrated poets
reclining inside the pressurized cabin,
flying over me on their way back and forth
between New York and San Francisco
to give thrilling readings to one another
and afterward sip Chablis and laugh
knowingly about books I've neither heard of nor read.
When they look down briefly at the Mississippi
they think of miserable James Wright
or miserable John Berryman,
or the strangely underwhelming poetry of Robert Bly.
Do they know the Microsoft of this little city
used to be that river, which powered the flour mills
that for some created great fortunes?
When I was young, one of the mills exploded
after a squatter ashed his cigarette,
and a transformative fire raged into a cold night.
When it was over we drove past the ruins
the fireman had encased in jagged sculptures of ice.
We sometimes still call this town Mill City
even though the last of the mills
have been converted into multi-million-dollar lofts
for retired financial services professionals,
with stainless steel restaurant-grade appliances,
and bathroom floors lined with hidden tubes
carrying hot water to keep their toes warm when they step from the tub.
This is how it can feel looking down at the river,
or last night up at the fragments of a space station shattering
as it reached the atmosphere, through binoculars
manufactured by people in China
who are not allowed to read such news on the Internet.
James Wright said Minneapolis is a horrible city
to commit suicide in because its waters are so often frozen.

I wonder whether he thought of those words
when he learned that John Berryman
had leapt from the Washington Avenue Bridge
onto the frozen ground of Bohemian Flats.
Later today my job, which is not the making of this poetry,
or the milling of flour, or the recovery of cosmic fragments
from the sea, will take me to the airport where strangers
will search my body and find nothing except this poem,
perhaps forgotten in my back pocket,
and after I tie my shoes I will share the concourse silently
with people who are passing through to other places,
and for as long as the moving sidewalk
pushes us past the cold windows
I'll delete tiny messages from my phone while moving
more quickly standing still than was once thought possible,
just enough clothes in my bag to get me back home.

No, You Turn

JASON GOOD

My first week in Minneapolis, I turned onto Lake Street and found myself heading the wrong direction on a one-way.

I raised my hand to indicate my guilt and offer apologies to the oncoming traffic. But instead of swerving around me, my new Minneapolis comrades did something I didn't expect.

They stopped.

And we idled there, all six of us, stalemated in the middle of the intersection—me with my hands above my head, mouthing "I'm sorry," and them with white knuckles and tight lips, their faces twisting to hide a festering rage.

"What is it that you want me to do, exactly?" I said to no one. Yes, I screwed up. Do we have to make a thing about it? Please, let it go. I have somewhere to be, and apparently need directions getting there.

A few weeks ago, I pulled out in front of a woman driving a Subaru station wagon. In my own defense, taking a left out of my local grocer's parking lot is always pretty dicey. Parked cars obstruct the view. The angle of oncoming traffic lands squarely in my blind spot.

And let me be clear: I only pulled out beside the Subaru driver into the adjacent lane. I was nowhere near her. Nonetheless, she recoiled as if accosted by a raccoon, and then proceeded to yell and point at me from the safety of her jaunty Outback.

I shrugged. Once again, I mouthed the words "I'm sorry!" But that wasn't enough. Her misplaced anger flailed against the driver's side window with the tenacity of a cat trying to exit a bathtub.

My family moved to Minneapolis a few years ago from New York City, where we lived for over a decade.

It had taken me a while to build up the courage to drive in Manhattan. Honestly, it seemed like a good way to end up in a neck brace. But I dug deep, did a little positive self-talk, and eventually found myself behind the wheel.

There, I found that drivers never slowed down or stopped unless it was absolutely necessary. But they used their turn signals. They let people in. They slowed down a little when it was snowing. There was a sense we were all in this together, the lunacy of driving on that crazy island grid. We accepted that other drivers made mistakes. We knew that sometimes the best option was to take a deep breath, step on the gas, and just go.

And look, I'm not an award-winning driver. In fact, my wife rarely lets me drive when our kids are in the car. This says about as much about my driving skills as it does about her personality.

But in those times when I am alone, and therefore permitted to commandeer our family-size vehicle, I have concluded that Minnesota drivers vibrate—often quite violently—between how they want to be perceived and how they really feel inside.

I've observed that each Minnesota driver has two personalities fighting inside them: "I'm an Outdoorsy Zen Nordic Type" and "I'm a Reckless Existentialist Swede."

That leaves drivers stuck in a psychologically tenuous state, causing them to behave erratically. They stop when they don't have a stop sign (Outdoorsy Zen). They rarely use their turn signals (Reckless Existentialist). They merge tentatively on the highway and drive too slowly in the left lane (Outdoorsy Zen). Or they drive too fast in the right, and entirely too fast on icy roads (Reckless Existentialist).

I'm left either sighing in disbelief at the snail's pace of traffic, or gasping in horror at how thoroughly I was dusted by that pick-up truck with a six-point buck strapped to its hood.

I would like to suggest to my fellow Minnesota drivers that it's okay—preferable, even—to get angry. And it's most effective to do so outside of your personal safety zone. After all, anger is a useful emotion. It focuses us. It burns calories and releases adrenaline.

But it's crucial that you channel the anger, spread it out a bit, have confidence that it's justified. Don't put the beast in a kennel all day and then unleash it while you're alone in the car.

In New York, there are plenty of ways to channel anger. Whether it's waiting for a delayed subway train, tripping over a refrigerator someone left on the sidewalk or slipping on someone's abandoned wig, there's always somewhere to focus your frustrations. Eventually you learn to accept, and even embrace, these wonderful opportunities to let off steam.

Maybe there just isn't enough juicy stuff to get mad about here in Minnesota. My neighborhood message board was recently jammed with people aghast over someone's decision to throw away, rather than donate, a futon mattress. It's no wonder people erupt with fury in their cars—they are the victims of a lack of opportunity.

So perhaps we should all get together and scream into each other's faces for a few minutes every day. How about we meet in the middle of the Hennepin-Lake intersection? It can't hurt, right?

Safe in Minnesota

AHMED ISMAIL YUSUF

My parents' land
The city of Ceerigaabo, with its endless spring water in summer
The lush mountains of Daalo, which touch the sea
The gorgeous, evergreen hills of Cal-madow
And Somalia's peaceful past
Are in my heart, where I hold them firm.

We are safe in Minnesota now
Safe as a soul in a house.
With its scenery of bridges supported by zoned pillars
With ten thousand alluring lakes
With the Mississippi's pouring, powerful current
Where neighbors so often show they care.

In the name of the gracefully affirmed
He who guards against all ill will
On whom books of all that knowledge are based
Surrounding students with he who guides.

The Revealing Season

MARLON JAMES

Moved to Minnesota in a warm and humid August. Moving for work because, well, what other reason does one move to the Midwest? But also because Macalester College hired me to teach creative writing full-time for one year. That job interview took place months before, in Philadelphia, a city I also did not know. A city that I took the bus to from New York, after flying in from Jamaica. An interview for a job I did not get. In fact, Macalester calling me back in the nick of time saved me from a near miss with Iowa. Because I was not one of their final candidates, I never came out to visit, and because I never came out to visit, the first time I saw Minnesota was the first time I showed up for work.

So back to work. But first a backtrack to Jamaica. I was supposed to leave the country for one year, but I packed as if leaving for good. This is a slightly different thing for a writer, meaning that when my friends saw that I was leaving behind all the furniture, appliances, and most of the clothes, but packing all my books, they knew I was never coming back.

Not that I planned to go off the grid, but I knew I was walking out of one life into another. But that makes this essay far too melodramatic far too early, and as I say to my students all the time, don't confuse melodrama with drama. But the point I'm making is that it wasn't so much that I was running to Minnesota, as I was running from Jamaica.

But many who run to Minnesota are running from something, and we date back even before the great migration, when black Americans ran from the Jim Crow South. It means that for many, myself included, summer in Minnesota means escape. And not always with drama attached.

Sometimes escape means a final reprieve from winter. We learn quickly that it never comes with spring, not with snow always threatening to fall, all the way into May. We are never truly in the clear until summer. You only really escape once, and if that was all there was to Minnesota I would have left years ago. We stay because summer promises something far greater and more enduring than escape: renewal.

Renewal happens on every level. Nature rewiring itself, regreening and regrowing itself, with everyone involved in a sort of statewide coming out. Summer is a bunch of specifics for many, lots of parks and lots of recreation, but it's a sum of abstractions for me. Themes, motifs, things that resonate on a deeper level, like renewal, growth, an annual, renewable second chance, or maybe just a chance to cycle forty miles and soak up badly needed vitamin D.

It makes sense to me that I would finally come out and live my most real self in Minnesota. That as summer opened up and showed itself, so would I. That it's not our infamous winters but our summers where Minnesota shows the truest version of herself.

And if you live here, you always feel as if you cheated into something wonderful you didn't quite deserve. The most beautifully green urban center, or the most cosmopolitan wildlife showcase you can encounter on two legs or two wheels. Or four, when I con my friends into driving me around.

Summer is when I remember why I live here, and why I could never live anywhere else.

Prince is Alive!
(And Lives in Minneapolis)

NEAL KARLEN

John Nelson turns sixty-nine today, and all the semiretired piano man wants for his birthday is to shoot some pool with his firstborn son. "He's real handy with a cue," says Prince, laughing, as he threads his old white Thunderbird through his old black neighborhood toward his old man's house. "He's so cool. The man knows what time it is."

Hard time is how life has traditionally been clocked in North Minneapolis; this is the place *Time* forgot twelve years ago when the magazine's cover trumpeted "The Good Life in Minnesota," alongside a picture of Governor Wendell Anderson holding up a walleye. Though tame and middle-class by Watts and Roxbury standards, the North Side offers some of the few mean streets in town.

The old sights bring out more Babbitt than Badass in Prince as he leads a leisurely tour down the main streets of his inner-city Gopher Prairie. He cruises slowly, respectfully: stopping completely at red lights, flicking on his turn signal even when no one's at an intersection. Gone is the wary kung fu Grasshopper voice with which Prince whispers when meeting strangers or accepting Academy Awards. Cruising peacefully with the window down, he's proof in a paisley jump suit that you can always go home again, especially if you never really left town.

Tooling through the neighborhood, Prince speaks matter-of-factly of why he toyed with early interviewers about his father and mother, their divorce, and his adolescent wanderings between the homes of his parents, friends, and relatives. "I used to tease a lot of journalists early on," he says, "because I wanted them to concentrate on the music and not so much on me coming from a broken home. I really didn't think that was important. What was important was what came out of my system that particular day. I don't live in the past. I don't play my old records for that reason. I make a statement, then move on to the next."

The early facts, for the neo-Freudians: John Nelson, leader of the Prince Rogers Trio, knew Mattie Shaw from North Side community dances. A singer sixteen years John's junior, Mattie bore traces of Billie Holiday in her pipes and more than a trace of Indian and Caucasian in her blood.

She joined the Prince Rogers Trio, sang for a few years around town, married John Nelson, and dropped out of the group. She nicknamed her husband after the band; the son who came in 1958 got the nickname on his birth certificate. At home and on the street, the kid was "Skipper." Mattie and John broke up ten years later, and Prince began his domestic shuttle.

"There's where my mom lives," he says nonchalantly, nodding toward a neatly trimmed house and lawn. "My parents live very close by each other, but they don't talk. My mom's the wild side of me; she's like that all the time. My dad's real serene; it takes the music to get him going. My father and me, we're one and the same." A wry laugh. "He's a little sick, just like I am."

Most of North Minneapolis has gone outside this Saturday afternoon to feel summer, that two-week season, locals joke, between winter and road construction. During this scenic tour through the neighborhood, the memories start popping faster. The Thunderbird turns left at a wooden two-story church whose steps are lined with bridesmaids in bonnets and ushers in tuxedos hurling rice up at a beaming couple framed in the door. "That was the church I went to growing up," says Prince. "I wonder who's getting married." A fat little kid waves, and Prince waves back.

"Just all kinds of things here," he goes on, turning right. "There was a school right there, John Hay. That's where I went to elementary school," he says, pointing out a field of black tar sprouting a handful of bent metal basketball rims. "And that's where my cousin lives. I used to play there every day when I was twelve, on these streets, football up and down this block. That's his father out there on the lawn."

These lawns are where Prince the adolescent would also amuse his friends with expert imitations of pro wrestlers Mad Dog Vachon and the Crusher. To amuse himself, he learned to play a couple dozen instruments. At thirteen, he formed Grand Central, his first band, with some high-school friends. Grand Central often traveled to local hotels and gyms to band-battle with their black competition: Cohesion, from the derided "bourgeois" South Side, and Flyte Tyme, which, with the addition of Morris Day, would later evolve into the Time.

Prince is fiddling with the tape deck inside the Thunderbird. On low volume comes his unreleased "Old Friends 4 Sale," an arrow-to-the-heart rock ballad about trust and loss. Unlike "Positively 4th Street"—which Bob Dylan reputedly named after a nearby Minneapolis block—the lyrics are sad, not bitter. "I don't know too much about Dylan," says Prince, "but I respect him a lot. 'All along the Watchtower' is my favorite of his. I heard it first from Jimi Hendrix."

"Old Friends 4 Sale" ends, and on comes "Strange Relationships," an as-yet-unreleased dance tune. "Is it too much?" asks Prince about playing his own songs in his own car. "Not long ago I was riding around LA with [a well-known rock star], and all he did was play his own stuff over and over. If it gets too much, just tell me."

He turns onto Plymouth, the North Side's main strip. When Martin Luther King got shot, it was Plymouth Avenue that burned. "We used to go to that McDonald's there," he says. "I didn't have any money, so I'd just stand outside there and smell stuff. Poverty makes people angry, brings out their worst side. I was very bitter when I was young. I was insecure and I'd attack anybody. I couldn't keep a girlfriend for two weeks. We'd argue about anything."

Across the street from McDonald's, Prince spies a smaller landmark. He points to a vacant corner phone booth and remembers a teenage fight with a strict and unforgiving father. "That's where I called my dad and begged him to take me back after he kicked me out," he begins softly. "He said no, so I called my sister and asked her to ask him. So she did, and afterward told me that all I had to do was call him back, tell him I was sorry, and he'd take me back. So I did, and he still said no. I sat crying at that phone booth for two hours. That's the last time I cried."

In the years between that phone booth breakdown and today's pool game came forgiveness. Says Prince, "Once I made it, got my first record contract, got my name on a piece of paper and a little money in my pocket, I was able to forgive. Once I was eating every day, I became a much nicer person." But it took many more years for the son to understand what a jazzman father needed to survive. Prince figured it out when he moved into his purple house.

"I can be upstairs at the piano, and Rande [his cook] can come in," he says. "Her footsteps will be in a different time, and it's real weird when you hear something that's a totally different rhythm than what you're playing. A lot of times that's mistaken for conceit or not having a heart. But it's not. And my dad's the same way, and that's why it was so hard for him to live with anybody. I didn't realize that until recently. When he was working or thinking, he had a private pulse going constantly inside him. I don't know, your bloodstream beats differently."

Prince pulls the Thunderbird into an alley behind a street of neat frame houses, stops behind a wooden one-car garage, and rolls down the window. Relaxing against a tree is a man who looks like Cab Calloway. Dressed in a crisp white suit, collar, and tie, a trim and smiling John Nelson adjusts his best cuff links and waves. "Happy birthday," says the son.

"Thanks," says the father, laughing. Nelson says he's not even allowing himself a piece of cake on his birthday. "No, not this year," he says with a shake of his head. Pointing at his son, Nelson continues, "I'm trying to take off ten pounds I put on while visiting him in Los Angeles. He eats like I want to eat, but he exercises, which I certainly don't."

Father then asks son if maybe he should drive himself to the pool game so he won't have to be hauled all the way back afterward. Prince says okay, and Nelson, chuckling, says to the stranger, "Hey, let me show you what I got for my birthday two years ago." He goes over to the garage and gives a tug on the door handle. Squeezed inside is a customized deep-purple BMW. On the rear seat is a copy of Prince's latest LP, *Around the World in a Day*. While the old man gingerly backs his car out, Prince smiles. "He never drives that thing. He's afraid it's going to get dented." Looking at his own white Thunderbird, Prince goes on: "He's always been that way. My father gave me this a few years ago. He bought it new in 1966. There were only 22,000 miles on it when I got it."

An ignition turns. "Wait," calls Prince, remembering something. He grabs a tape off the Thunderbird seat and yells to his father, "I got something for you to listen to. Lisa [Coleman] and Wendy [Melvoin] have been working on these in LA." Prince throws the tape, which the two female members of his band had mixed, and his father catches it with one hand. Nelson nods okay and pulls his car behind his son's in the alley. Closely tailing Prince through North Minneapolis, he waves and smiles whenever we look back. It's impossible to believe that the gun-toting geezer in *Purple Rain* was modeled after John Nelson.

"That stuff about my dad was part of [director-cowriter] Al Magnoli's story," Prince explains. "We used parts of my past and present to make the story pop more, but it was a story. My dad wouldn't have nothing to do with guns. He never swore, still doesn't, and never drinks." Prince looks in his rearview mirror at the car tailing him. "He don't look sixty-nine, do he? He's so cool. He's got girlfriends, lots of 'em." Prince drives alongside two black kids walking their bikes. "Hey, Prince," says one casually. "Hey," says the driver with a nod, "how you doing?"

Passing by old neighbors watering their lawns and shooting hoops, the North Side's favorite son talks about his hometown. "I wouldn't move, just cuz I like it here so much. I can go out and not get jumped on. It feels good not to be hassled when I dance, which I do a lot. It's not a thing of everybody saying, 'Whoa, who's out with who here?' while photographers flash their bulbs in your face."

Nearing the turnoff that leads from Minneapolis to suburban Eden Prairie, Prince flips in another tape and peeks in the rearview mirror. John Nelson is still right behind. "It's real hard for my father to show emotion," says Prince, heading onto the highway. "He never says 'I love you,' and whenever we try to hug or something, we bang our heads together like in some Charlie Chaplin movie. But a while ago, he was telling me how I always had to be careful. My father told me, 'If anything happens to you, I'm gone.' All I thought at first was that it was a real nice thing to say. But then I thought about it for a while and realized something. That was my father's way of saying 'I love you.'"

A few minutes later, Prince and his father pull in front of the Warehouse, a concrete barn in an Eden Prairie industrial park. Inside, the Family, a rock-funk band that Prince has begun working with, is pounding out new songs and dance routines. The group is as tight as ace drummer Jellybean Johnson's pants. At the end of one hot number, Family members fell on their backs, twitching like fried eggs.

Prince and his father enter to hellos from the still-gyrating band. Prince goes over to a pool table by the soundboard, racks the balls, and shimmies to the beat of the Family's next song. Taking everything in, John Nelson gives a professional nod to the band, his son's rack job, and his own just-chalked cue. He hitches his shoulders, takes aim, and breaks like Minnesota Fats. A few minutes later, the band is still playing and the father is still shooting. Prince, son to this father and father to this band, is smiling.

(First published 1985)

Bobby Zimmerman was Here

LEIF PETTERSEN

In the summer of 1960, my then fifteen-year-old father, Cleve Pettersen, went to Radio Shack and bought one of the first commercially available, portable reel-to-reel tape recorders. The thing was the size of a small ottoman and weighed about as much as a boulder of the same dimensions. It cost $50, which is over $400 in today's economy, so not an insignificant purchase for a fifteen-year-old.

My dad had befriended a precocious kid from his neighborhood, Bil Golfus, who had inserted himself into the Dinkytown coffeehouse music scene. He'd tagged along on a few of Golfus's outings, crossing paths with several musicians, including "Spider" John Koerner, Tony Glover, and the late Dave Ray, who banded together to release albums under the name "Koerner, Ray, and Glover."

Inspired by the field work of John and Alan Lomax, who traveled the South recording and preserving American folk music for the Library of Congress in the 1930s and 1940s (they famously installed a "state-of-the-art" 300-pound wire recorder in the trunk of their Ford sedan), Dad resolved to record some Dinkytown performers for posterity. Alas, none of the musicians in the scene felt inclined to indulge a fifteen-year-old aspiring archivist, with the exception of one—nineteen-year-old Bob Dylan.

The previous fall, Dylan had arrived in Minneapolis from the iron range, ostensibly to attend the University of Minnesota. By all accounts, he didn't get to class often, instead choosing to spend most of his time attached to his guitar. He first lived in an apartment overlooking the alley above Gray's Drugstore, on the corner of Fourteenth Avenue SE and Fourth Street in Dinkytown. He later moved a few blocks away to an unremarkable, two-story, multi-unit building with bay windows at 711 Fifteenth Avenue SE.

Apart from vacant university desk chairs, Dylan's time in Minneapolis was marked by honing his growing passion for folk and blues music and playing small gigs in coffee shops. After he'd morphed himself from Bobby Zimmerman to "Bob Dylan," but before he'd begun composing original music in earnest, he made a recording that was reverently known for decades as the *Minneapolis Party Tape*.

Dinkytown's folk performers were mostly interchangeable, performing the same songs with roughly the same delivery, my dad recalls. Among this crowd, Dylan wasn't considered to be one of the best, but the upside was he had a burning curiosity to hear what he sounded like while performing. Dylan wasn't his top choice, he was simply grateful college kids had agreed to briefly let him into their circle.

So, one afternoon my dad and Golfus lugged that beast of a tape recorder to Dylan's ground-floor apartment on Fifteenth Avenue SE (the asbestos-filled building was demolished in 2014), for a living room jam session. Also present at the "party" was girlfriend Bonnie Beecher (who would one day marry Grateful Dead/Woodstock character Wavy Gravy) and friend Cynthia Fisher.

Over the course of roughly two hours, as Bob, Bonnie, and Cynthia demolished a bottle of wine, they recorded twelve songs, about thirty-one minutes in total length. All the songs were covers by artists like Woody Guthrie and Jimmie Rodgers, including "Come See Jerusalem," "I Thought I Heard That Casey When She Blowed" and "I'm Gonna Walk the Streets of Glory." There's also a one-minute original song Bob wrote commemorating the laziness of his roommate, Hugh Brown.

Dylan wasn't Dylan yet. "If you don't know it's Dylan," my dad said decades later, "you think it's someone pretending to be Dylan and not doing a good job." However, being one of the first recordings he ever made, it's considered a landmark Dylan artifact, and serves as a small, priceless progress report on Dylan's musical development. He wouldn't make any professional quality recordings until two years later.

The recording is sometimes rough and tinny, though surprisingly clear at other times. Back-chat and ambient noise can be heard between some songs as well as a genial Dylan trading barbs with Cynthia during "Liberty Ship." Bob coughs quite a bit during and between songs. As the room peppers him with suggestions about what to sing next, Bob is tentative, oddly unsure about which songs will sound good on a recording.

Dylan frequently stopped so they could rewind and listen to what he'd just recorded, which is how they discovered that the first few songs suffered from poor sound quality due to table vibrations from the coffee table the microphone was sitting on. After that, Dad simply held the mic in front of Dylan for the remainder of the session, and the quality improved. When they'd finished, Dylan asked to rewind and listen to the entire recording one more time, then Dad and Golfus left. Dad never saw Dylan again.

By December of the same year, Dylan abandoned college and made his way to New York's Greenwich Village. Within the year, he had a contract with Columbia Records and his skyrocketing fame had begun.

For years, the *Minneapolis Party Tape* languished in obscurity. A few rough copies had been made, but most hardcore Dylanologists hadn't heard the seminal recording until 2005, when Dad donated the original tape to the Minnesota Historical Society. The tape isn't on display, but CD and cassette copies of the tape are available to be checked out and listened to—onsite only, no copying allowed.

Coincidentally, Dad's donation happened just in time for Dylan's people to catch wind of the news and include some of the *Minneapolis Party Tape* music in the 2005 Martin Scorsese documentary *No Direction Home*. One of these tracks, "Rambler, Gambler," was also included on *The Bootleg Series, Vol. 7: No Direction Home* collection. This late contribution earned Dad an invitation to the film's premiere in New York.

In my own years as a travel writer, I've told this story to people all across the world, who've listened rapt and wide-eyed. People who actually know the legend of the *Minneapolis Party Tape* go particularly bananas, as if they're traveling back through time and touching the essence of young Dylan through my words. The subtext is often, "Who would've known that Minneapolis was more than a bleak, scrappy tundra, even in the early sixties?" We usually don't get musical credit until the era of Prince and the Replacements, and then only grudgingly.

We may not be renowned, but Minneapolis's history as a percolator of brilliance runs deep. Bobby Zimmerman may not have achieved greatness in Minneapolis, but the city undeniably pointed him in that direction before he headed down Highway 61, past the town of Rollingstone, and into history, taking me and my dad along for the ride.

Rock 'n' Roll Exterminators

ERIC DREGNI

In the early nineties, my two bandmates and I took a vow of poverty just to play music in Minneapolis. Our city had earned the unfortunate nickname of "Murderapolis," but we fooled ourselves that we were loyal to our hometown while other musicians fled to Seattle. In fact, we just couldn't afford to go.

Wasn't Minneapolis the musical center of the world? The Witch's Hat Tower near Dinkytown supposedly inspired Dylan to write "All Along the Watchtower," the Ramones saw signs for "Cretin Avenue" in St. Paul and penned the punk rock anthem "Cretin Hop," and of course Prince sang about "Uptown" where he zoomed through on his purple motorcycle. My bandmates and I had a revelation at the Stardust Lanes in the Hub of Hell neighborhood that revealed our band's name: Vinnie and the Stardüsters.

New York was impossibly expensive for musicians and Minneapolis had the one essential ingredient for rock 'n' roll: basements. Only in this literal underground could our fair city breed an unparalleled indie rock scene with regular concerts by the likes of the Replacements, Babes in Toyland, Soul Asylum, the Jayhawks, and Hüsker Dü, but the real gems were the lesser known bands: Lily Liver, Jan, DeFormo, Rank Strangers, Swing Set, TVBC, Urban Guerrillas, Boiled in Lead, Kruddler, Walt Mink, the Sandwiches, Götterdämmerung, and dozens of others—but not The Cows (they were terrible).

We ignored the hazards of blasting music below ground level. The chipping lead paint (it has a sweet flavor), the sprinkling asbestos from the heating ducts (like shimmering stardust), the diseased vermin scurrying underfoot, and the radioactive radon seeping through the floor couldn't kill invincible musicians. Instead, our main obstacle was paying the rent on almost no income.

We packed our squalid rental houses full of sketchy musicians. In a little Grand Avenue bungalow, our drummer Nick rented a front hall closet for $50 a month that was just large enough for his single mattress and his clothes hung above his head. The payoff was that we could play music in the basement. When his housemates raised the rent for Nick's closet to $75 a month, he moved his bed into his tan Subaru station wagon, so he could sleep wherever he wanted. "I can just park right outside of my job. I can sleep until the last minute and go right to work," he bragged. "The only trouble is bathing. Luckily I have lots of friends with showers."

Even after Nick moved out, we continued to practice in the house. He didn't know anyone who lived there anymore and the scary new residents gave us strange looks. One day, however, the front door was sealed shut and a note stated that the St. Paul Police shut down this crack house.

I moved in with my brother Jonathan who had recently traded his Haight-Ashbury look from his Deadhead days in San Francisco for a partially shaved head and T-shirts silk screened with a large encircled "A." For some reason, he had a large collection of bowling balls, but no interest in the sport. I soon discovered that he'd joined the "Revolutionary Anarchist Bowling League" (RABL), some of whom lobbed bowling balls through windows of Army recruiters.

My brother's tactic for surviving was shopping at the Red Owl across the street for the cheapest food by the pound: onions, split peas, lots of cabbage, but mostly creamed corn. He boiled the big mess in a giant pot and the gaseous vapors swirled through our rental house and permanently stained the countertop or anything it touched. He bought numerous appliances, especially several toasters, for pennies at the Goodwill outlet, Diggers, to help change his diet from the gut-wrenching soup. "If a toaster breaks, I'll just grab another one from the garage," he reasoned.

With all the bowling balls, toasters, and mystery soups, I wondered if I shouldn't be roommates with my brother. My suspicions were confirmed when I noticed him cutting holes in his thick foam mattress. He explained that his cat didn't like to get her paws wet or dirty in the litter box, so the sweet feline had taken to peeing on his mattress that soaked up any liquid. He couldn't find another replacement at Diggers, so his mattress looked like Swiss cheese.

I then moved into a house with five guys with a large, filthy basement perfect for band practice. I didn't have a guitar, so I borrowed one from my friend Scott, whose brother took the photo of his swimming baby for the cover of Nirvana's *Nevermind* album. I imagined that this fame would rub off on our band. The next day, though, one of the roommates named Chank left the backdoor open to air out the grease fumes from his daily hamburgers fried in an inch of fat. Fresh air poured in along with mice and music thieves who plundered our instruments. I was forced to find new friends to lend us their musical instruments, and our chance to ride on Nirvana's coattails was squandered.

The mice burrowed right through my laundry bag and out the other side. I couldn't afford new clothes, so I wore the holey ones, hoping to finally be in style when I noticed the new catalog from Macy's featuring trendy "Grunge Wear" pre-ruined outfits. Suddenly our poverty was chic. The mice didn't chew my clothes in the "right" places, however, leaving holes that sometimes left intimate parts of my body exposed.

My roommate Willy recommended his dubious method to "procure" (steal) better clothes. Rather than loading up on bowling balls at the Goodwill, as my brother Jonathan did, Willy wore his worst clothes there. He chose nicer clothes, changed in the dressing room, and simply left his old clothes behind as he walked out of the store in his new outfit.

I couldn't in good conscience follow Willy's lead, so I considered shopping at Diggers, which sold clothes by the pound. Then our friend Lula warned that she was scouting for good second-hand clothes for her vintage clothing store and spotted a good-looking young man digging through the bins. "There are *never* cute guys at Diggers," she told me. Just as she was about to say "Hi," she noticed him pull out an old woman's shoe, rip up the insole, and shove it into his face, sniffing violently.

Our singer John offered me advice when he saw my mouse-eaten clothes. He sympathized since he had a vermin infestation where he lived at the "Halfway House," named for its location halfway between the dingy C. C. Club and the fabulously kitschy Black Forest Inn. Here's how he beat the mice: "I just take all the empty beer cases and line the walls with them." The entire kitchen at the Halfway House had boxes of returnable bottles from floor to ceiling. "It makes the room much smaller but keeps out mice, cockroaches, and even works as insulation."

Nick boasted that he didn't have to worry about mice in his Subaru, the movable bedroom, but the frigid winter forced him to rent an actual room in a house on Lyndale Avenue. Since he needed rent money, he strategically parked his beat-up station wagon sticking out from the curb near a patch of ice. Late one night, a car bashed into his Subaru. He rushed outside to write down the license plate and reported the hit-and-run to the police. He cashed in, paid his rent, and helped fund the recording of the first Stardüsters' single.

One morning while we were practicing at Nick's house, his roommate Andrew wandered into the kitchen to search for something to eat. The fridge was empty except for an old bottle of Tabasco. A convenience store was directly across the street from the house, but the roommate was too hungry—or perhaps too lazy—to venture out to buy something to eat.

Instead he took a few sheets of paper towels, sprinkled the hot sauce on top and ate them. When we came out of the practice space, the roommate was finishing up the last of the quilted paper towels with little floral patterns.

We practiced in Nick's basement, but another roommate had tried to solve their rodent problem by leaving rat poison in every corner. The mice died by the dozens in the walls of the house and their putrid stench made band practice there impossible.

We moved our equipment to the house of our friend Rog, from the band Full Metal Hangover. His roommate, Tony, had a ferret to rout out all the mice in his house, but the stench of this animal, mixed with the mildew in the basement, made us have to leave the windows wide open to let in the freezing fresh air. The smell disappeared and the mice returned when Tony and the ferret moved out. Soon after, Tony was elected as a Minnesota state senator.

Meanwhile, John's pest problem resurfaced since he had to return the empty beer boxes to the liquor store to get the rent money from the deposit on the bottles. His roommate brought home a cat to catch mice. One night, John was awakened by the sounds of pained howling. He woke up his roommate and together they noticed a small red bubble emerging from the cat's rear. They carefully inspected the feline's derriere and deduced that the poor thing had ingested a used condom and was having trouble passing the tasty morsel. To help the suffering feline, the roommate held the cat while John gripped the latex bubble with pliers. John yanked with all his might but lost his grip on the pliers. The semi-digested condom snapped back, causing the poor cat to yelp. Eventually the rubber wiggled free. The cat hid for a week but continued to scrounge for discarded treats.

Back in my house, Chank found two kittens to keep out mice. The cats, however, were far more interested in his hamburger pan and just followed the meat mist that was visible in the air when he cooked. Chank refused to remove the inch of grease from the pan caused by cooking burgers twice a day, and sometimes dropped in shots of 151 rum into the sizzling mass. When guests arrived, he dropped in a lit match for "hamburger flambé" and set off the smoke alarms as a soundtrack.

I decided I'd rather live with rodents than those worthless fat cats. Then one day we realized that we had always had the resolution within our grasp. During practice in the basement, Nick bought a new deafening Zildjian ride cymbal; John and I turned up our amps as loud as possible to compensate. The windows rattled, the joists shook, my roommates shouted for us to turn down, and a mouse fell from the ceiling of the basement, dead.

Spark

VALÉRIE DÉUS

We're going to run
all over this city tonight

every one way
every full stop

brown girls in skirts
create the black light

while the helix haired
barter in hugs

drum dreamers thrive
in the afterglow

while shadows
interrupt the grain

eating cheese curds
how 'bout you?

There's a funnel cake
in my future puzzle

hippies still preaching love
even with the weather report
crawling all over this ultraviolet night

A man declares
his soul surrenders to the dark side
and I believe him
I mean, he's nothing to
his puppet leaders

bugs attracted to the brights
sticking to the glass

others hang back in the black
See? We all hate standing in the light

with a breeze coming in from the west
that last kiss wasn't intentional

It's my knees
I lose them to smiles on bikes
their locs illuminated by the dawn

Wild Places

KELLY BARNHILL

When I was a kid, there were always a lot of people in my house. Relatives. Visitors. With kids. And sometimes my mom would watch the kids who were related to us and those who weren't. I was the oldest of five children— which is a lot—but there were always extra kids. Just hanging around. My mom always seemed on the edge of losing her mind, a fact that frustrated me at the time, but now makes total sense.

"Out," she'd say, once she found the strength within her to be capable of speech. "*This minute.*"

The subtext was, in every case, completely clear: I was *in charge*, and really should keep everyone away from the house until it looked like the walls were no longer holding their breath. So I did what any oldest child would do in that situation. I told stories. I made up games. And I took them over to the park.

There are some things that you are going to need to know in order for all of this to make sense. First, you should know that I have a lot of relatives. Like, a *lot*. Cousins and second cousins and maybe third? I'm pretty sure that's a thing. And brothers and sisters and uncles and aunts and other adults who we always called *Uncle Something* or *Aunt Something*, but were really some other sort of relation that doesn't really need its own distinction once you come down to it. Growing up, my sense of the word *family* was expansive and uncontained. It was not a thing with borders on it.

Second, you should know this: Being the oldest child of a large family—the oldest child of a large, *Catholic* family—always had its own level of *extra*. Plus I was a girl. Which meant that I had, from a very young age, certain responsibilities. I was, to use the local parlance, *in charge*. In the playroom. In the basement. In the backyard. I had responsibilities: to mind, protect, and admonish, within reason, and to provide entertainments. That's what it meant to be *in charge*. I was tasked with taking the younger children to the library, or to their friends' houses, or up and down the sidewalk on their big wheels, or to the park. It's the park that I want to talk about now. Or not the park, exactly.

The gap behind the park.

There is one more thing you should know. I grew up in Minneapolis, a city that has, for much of its history, tried desperately to pretend that it is something it's not. Unnatural, perfectly straight lines drawn across bog and swampland, angles and edges where there should be none. A city built on a nonexistent firmament, a pile of dry dirt and gravel poured onto ancient mud holes and peat bogs. A city that lounges on the man-made beaches of dredged-out lakes, under the shade of non-native trees. It is a city that, in the Protestant tradition, attempted a façade of rationality and order—a perfect grid of right angles and regular blocks and streets with numbers or bearing the alphabetized names of mustachioed men who had, once upon a time, Achieved Great Things.

And yet.

Despite this civilly engineered precision, there are gaps here and there, where wildness seeps out. The bog teases and bulges under the streets until they crack. Sidewalks buckle. Basements weep and spall. Muck and water and tangled green asserts itself between the straight streets and rigid curbs, and sometimes, here and there, a little tangled wood emerges in the gaps. These gaps are magical places—geographically small, and yet. The space within feels uncontained. And limitless. And I was, once upon a time, extraordinarily good at finding these gaps. Each time when we were banished from the house, I would lead the children to the gap below the park.

This gap was a strip of woods near our house. Actually, "woods" is a bit of an exaggeration. In truth it was just the narrow remains of what was once a trolley line, abandoned in the fifties in our city's embrace of car culture, and had become a dense tangle of buckthorn and cottonwood and thick vines and tall grass. It sat above a lake and below a Greek Orthodox church. The church had stained glass the color of water, and a bright yellow dome, resting on its shoulders, like a bisected sun.

At the center of these woods were the rusting remains of old trolley tracks. The tracks were not always visible. Time had warped and broken the old ties and we had to watch our feet, as the nails stuck up out of the grass. The rails snaked in and out of the dirt, disappearing for a few yards, and then breaking free again. We used to put our hands on the old rails and swear on our lives that we could feel the vibrations of the trolleys that passed years and years ago. Or the trolleys that were here, even now, in a world that we couldn't see or touch but was real all the same. Fairy trains. Ghost trolleys. Overlaid realities and intersecting timelines. Seemed likely as anything else.

The woods were only a few blocks long and a couple hundred feet wide, but to us, they were the deep, dark woods of a fairy tale. It was quiet in there. And alive. You could hear the moss on the old stones breathing. Outside the woods, it was streets and paved paths and mowed lawns and parking lots as far as the eye could see—but within its ragged borders, it was shadow and blossom and loam and green. It was, hands down, my favorite place in the world.

One day, I led my little brother, a cousin, and a neighbor down into the scrub. I was in charge. They all had matching bright blonde heads and looked so similar you had to squint to tell them apart.

I was conducting business as usual—telling them about the monster that lived in what was once known as Lake Calhoun (now Bde Maka Ska). I told them that when the waves went dark and the world went quiet, it slithered out of the lake in the middle of the night, and how they had to make sure they kept their feet tucked into their blankets because the monster might come in their rooms and eat their toes. I told them that the rocks had ears and that the trolley platform was actually a portal to another world. I told them about the complicity of the trees in the capture and corralling of little boys for the Lake People who lived in the muck at the bottom of the water (this was mostly to discourage them from going feral and peeing on the tree trunks) and how if they weren't very careful, they would have to spend their days working on a seaweed farm, deep under the waves. The trees began swaying and creaking as I told this story. I will swear to you that one of them, very clearly, groaned, "Watch it, bub," to the neighbor kid.

When I turned around to show them the glinting bits of colored glass, shining like gems in the dirt, all of a sudden, there was a rustle and a breath of cold air, and all three boys were gone.

Gone.

I looked everywhere—the old drain pipe, the tall grasses, the gap behind the crumbling platform stairs. I ran from one end of the path to the other. I scrambled up the old platform stairs to the little playground at the church. I called their names. I called *so loud.* But the boys had vanished. I walked around the church, looked in the trees, scoured the steep hillside, and looked under each car parked on the road below.

This wasn't the first time this sort of thing had happened in those woods. Space was strange there. Time, too. I would sometimes go in there to read my book or write in my notebook and would swear that I had only been there for a minute or two when I had actually stayed all day. Another time I went there fully intended to run away from home, live on the rusty rails and tangled weeds forever—and honestly thought I had been there for days, only to come home later unmissed and unnoticed, discovering that I had only stayed in the shadows for perhaps a quarter of an hour. We already know that space-time is more twisted threads than straight lines—and perhaps we are simply more cognizant of this when we are children. Or perhaps there are places where the warbles and loops assert themselves. Perhaps that is what makes a gap.

I scrambled up the hill, to a partial courtyard at the Orthodox Church, which had a statue in the center of a fountain. The statue was a woman with one head and two bodies, connected at the neck. One body crouched by the water. The other had been unhooked from gravity and was flying away. I wondered if this is what happened to the three boys. Had they become unhooked too? Were they, right now, flying away? I called their names again. Only birds called back.

After an hour, I sank to the ground and began to cry. I didn't know what had happened. I feared the worst—that maybe the most terrifying bits and pieces of my own stories were actually true. Maybe their toes had been eaten by beasts. Maybe they had been captured by Lake People. Maybe they had become trees.

And then, with a loud yell, the boys came thundering back. They appeared all at once, on the tracks, tearing towards me like a train. They were crying, all of them. Their hands and knees were grubby. They had muddy tear stains on their faces. They told me that they ran back and forth and back and forth on the path, calling my name. They put their hands on the trolley tracks, checking for vibrations (the tracks, they said and still say, were warm and pulsing as though the trolley was nearly on top of them).

"I called for you," I told them, "but you were gone." "We called for you," they told me, "but you were gone." All of us were telling the truth.

We held hands very tightly.

We scrambled out of the woods.

I washed their faces and brought them home.

None of us ever told our mothers.

On Minnehaha Creek in May

KRIS BIGALK

When the willows are so new
they glow, letting their hair down
as they bend to the creek,
lowering their limbs into the water
whirling in spiral, a dance
I didn't quite remember—
this is the day when each second
raises another gnat from the mud,
when each sun-soaked minute
sears itself into the buds,
when each hour
brings us a little closer to sunset,
to the moment
when we press our bodies together,
warm against the dew
as night rises, the gnats settle,
and the willows bend towards us, listening.

Run for Me

LINDSAY NIELSEN

Neville's words spilled across my screen: "My world is closing in on me a bit too much these days. Would you be kind enough to take me with you on your next run?"

Neville lived in England, but wouldn't have been able to come running with me in person, even if he lived down the block. Diabetes was ravaging his body. As an older man, he was now an amputee, blind and wheelchair-bound. He told me early on in our relationship that his running days were over.

I understood his request; sometimes the only thing that works is a run. It had taken me twenty-five years since becoming an amputee myself to find my way back to running. The journey wasn't smooth because running on a prosthetic leg is a complicated affair. It was my need for information from other amputee runners that led me to the Amputee Listserv, where I found Neville.

Neville had drawn me out with questions about my experiences as an amputee. I began sharing droplets of thought and feeling, and soon the trickle became a flow. I'd never before talked openly about how I experienced the world as a person with a disability. I had passed as a biped for decades because I could. Joining the listserv was the beginning of my process of "coming out" as an amputee. I was just beginning to understand what passing had cost me.

"Yes, definitely, we can go for a run together!" I replied. "Do you care where we go?"

His response was immediate: "Anywhere in Minneapolis. Maybe to your beloved lake?"

***

The next afternoon, I headed out the door for our run. When I got back, I sat down at my computer, still damp with sweat, and started writing:

Dear Neville,
My watch reads 2:00 p.m. as I leave our blue-gray, flat-roofed house. The bright autumn sun touches my face while my pup whines at the window as I leave him behind.

I walk first to warm up my muscles, although walking on my running leg is awkward because my Flexfoot, shaped like the back leg of a cheetah, is designed for speed, not saunter. I breathe deeply. A hint of rosemary rides in on the breeze. As I round the corner, I see the herb garden sharing her scent. The plants are beautiful, but miniscule compared to England's offerings.

Years ago, I planted my first herbs with lush picture-book images of English hedges directing my shovel. I was too naïve to understand the full impact of our Minnesota climate. I spent many dollars and hours buying and planting lavender and rosemary along the path to our house. I wanted to smell their fragrance every time the kids brushed past. We have a short growing season here, and all too soon the Minnesota freeze came and put the meager plants out of their misery. But the long winter months blurred my memory so every spring I started all over, visions of English hedges once again driving my spade. Life lessons are embedded in gardening, as they are in sports. Like signing up for a race, the very act of planting is hopeful.

A few months after our fourteen-year-old son died, I found my way back into the garden even though it was hard to reattach to the outside world. While death took up most of my consciousness, I dug holes in the earth, sprinkled in seeds and watered them with no confidence they would survive. And just as the sun continued to rise every day, those tiny plantings poked their heads up through the earth and reminded me that life goes on, whether I was open to it or not. The force of life surprised me in those quiet hours, encompassed my grief, and ultimately healed me.

The Serenity Prayer was one of the first things I learned to recite when I got sober at twenty-one, and like everything else of substance, it was easier to memorize than integrate. "God, grant me the serenity to accept the things I cannot change, courage to change the things I can, and wisdom to know the difference." Decades later, I remain more courageous than wise, and acceptance only makes a reluctant appearance after every other possibility is exhausted.

Back to our run. As I make my way along the street, the leaves dance under my feet, crunching as they return to dust. They are just a smidgen past peak. The leaves' colors are intense in their assembly of reds, oranges, and yellows. I hear the sounds of the fat squirrels scampering up and down the trees. They are already gathering staples even though winter is technically six weeks away. Bird whistles and chirps fill the air, and a sense of happiness fills me all the way to my nonexistent toes. If Minnesota only had this one season, everyone would move here.

I begin to run. My left foot, the mechanical one, slaps the asphalt, while my right makes almost no sound at all. My cobalt blue windbreaker rustles. Reverberations climb up my legs, making their way into my hips. My arms swing, but I have been coached well enough not to let them cross the midline.

My breaths increase but remain rhythmic. The path takes me along Minnehaha Creek until I reach the place where the water tumbles upon itself trying to get through the iron grate in its rush for the lake.

I cross the street to the lake path. The Minneapolis skyline rises up in the distance but in just a few steps, city life fades away. Waves lap against the shore, water and rocks creating a complex melody. A crow screeches so loudly, I jump.

Sunlight reaches down through the wispy clouds, kissing the lake, causing a sparkle to explode across the surface. Large ducks with emerald heads and bright orange feet land, skidding across the water until they join the duck groups already floating. I scan the water's edge for my favorite great blue heron, but this late in the day, she's nowhere to be seen.

My feet pick up speed and my legs follow. Inside my single running shoe, my toes grab at the ground with every other step. Oxygen moves through my body with more force, breaths still rhythmic but now with a hint of rasp. I forgot to use my inhaler, so air travels over a rough spot in my lungs. My nose starts to run. I pull down the sunglasses still perched on my head and slip them into place on the bridge of my nose.

I plug one side of my nose, turn my head, and give a quick blow.

I continue along the path, closing in on a golden retriever and her owner, who asks to see my running prosthesis and tells me he finds himself inspired by my running.

Like a lot of challenged athletes, I have mixed feelings about "being inspiring." There are definitely times I feel honored because we all need to inspire as much as we need to be inspired. But I wonder how often this kind of inspiration truly evolves into change for the inspired. It annoys me when people squander ability, even though I do, too. Does this piss you off, Neville? As parts of your body have succumbed to the diabetes, do you get impatient when you hear others, me included, whine about lesser and oftentimes self-imposed limitations?

I push these thoughts aside. I made a deal with myself when I started running again that I would do my best to stay positively connected to nature and to people as a way to quiet my mind. At times, though, it's difficult to let myself just feel the vulnerability that comes with all that connection.

***

As I get close to finishing the lake, I increase my speed until I hit a full-blown sprint. I'm on my toes and hit the ground for the merest of touches. My breath *comes in gasps; my arms pump, forcing my feet to turn over more quickly, and I focus on keeping my gait even.*

I walk the last block home, letting my heart rate slow, noticing that the sun has moved toward the west. We've started the slide into shorter days. Soon I'll begin and end my runs before the sun even rises. I walk slowly past my own herb garden to the back door, tired but not hurting. I love the times when my leg doesn't rebel against the run.

Thank you for this shared adventure, Neville. It's so great to notice out loud what I often don't notice that I'm noticing. My life would be so much less without you, my friend—Linds

***

A little more than a year later, after Neville and I had four seasons of runs, my inbox held a new note, this from his son: "My father died this week. Thank you for being one of his friends, and for giving him mobility, if only in his mind."

Every year since Neville's passing, I take an autumn run or walk with my friend who continues to coach me to pay attention to the world I'm still lucky enough to inhabit. I feel his spirit dancing among the falling leaves, and sometimes in those moments, I find the serenity to accept the things I cannot change.

My Brother's Bachelor Party

KEVIN KLING

My brother is getting married, so his pals and I decide to throw a bachelor party. We convene at the bowling alley for an intensive planning session. At first the thoughts are simple and heartfelt—a few close friends, some cigars, a fine peppermint schnapps perhaps—but in a relatively short period of time we are huddled around a ballpoint pen and a map of Minneapolis, charting a downtown tour of Mephistophelian proportions. Over the din of shattering pins, one of the more lucid voices cries, "We should make a day of it. I know where we can get a school bus to take us."

On the morning of the big day we reconvene. There is an enthusiasm in the air, something is going to happen today, something certainly to relate and embellish time and again during cold evenings at the pub. These are the moments one feels the tingle that he is about to do something he ought to know better than, perhaps requiring stitches.

As we await the guest of honor, one of our members, who answers to the title "Lumper," dashes from his automobile, pale and breathless. He relates my brother is presently recovering at the hospital after receiving a horrific dog bite.

Good god, a dog bite. I recall with horror my own brush with a cur which went by the breed Weimariner. A hoary beast, without provocation or warning, lunged at me from behind a shrub. I felt the tingle of brutish teeth lodge in my calf. I have since learned this specific breed of dog, Weimariner, was developed in nineteenth-century Germany as a hunting companion, more specifically to bring down male deer by their genitalia. I now regard my brush as rather fortunate, accounts all taken, and have avoided the breed with the respect due its purpose.

But my brother, good god, a dog bite.

"Where? How? What dog?"

"His own dog," replied Lumper.

His dog—my brother's dog is a happy, slobbering Springer Spaniel. Wouldn't hurt a fly if it were wearing a bacon jacket and slacks.

"No, his dog was in a scrap with another dog. When Steven tried to separate the combatants, his dog, thinking it was the throat of the other dog, bit his ankle, leaving a healthy gash requiring eight to twelve stitches at last count."

A feasible explanation. While his dog was friend to all men, the creature held a great contempt for his own species, a fault I fear of premature weaning and a neglect of early socialization. We can learn much from the animal kingdom.

"Quick man, what hospital?"

We load into our charabanc and proceed toward the hospital. We find my brother patched and paid for and pleased that his chums were all frothed in the matter of his immediate release.

We head to the Hubert H. Humphrey Metrodome baseball arena, the boys amusing themselves in the back of the bus with a rousing game of, "Does This Hurt More, or Less?" We take our assigned seats and discover we have been placed quite a distance from the center of the action. Some of the lads have brought their baseball catching gloves, in hopes of snagging an errant home run. The banner marking "The furthest ball ever hit in the dome" is some fifteen rows in front of us. The likelihood of a free souvenir appears rather nil.

This does nothing to dowse our enthusiasm. Quite the contrary, we shout and cheer. We have come to have fun, by heavens, and brought plenty of our own friends so as not to be under any obligation to make new ones. Our enthusiasm is quickly met with a brace of barrel-chested ushers. We all put on our best behavior and settle into a meal of tubular cuisine *mitt kraut*.

The Twins' baseball match has hit a dull stretch. Also, our morning imbibing has worn off and we have "turned the corner," transforming us into a rather surly collection of revelers. We're bored, and when my brother is bored, no amount of beefed-up security is going to prevent something from happening.

Suddenly he says, "You see that kid?" He points several rows down where perch a twosome of adolescent boys, greedily helping themselves to a variety of unhealthy complexion-ravaging foodstuffs.

"Five bucks says when that kid is done with his nachos, he licks his cheese compartment."

A wager! Money immediately makes its way out of pockets.

"Yeah, I'm in for five."

"Yeah, me too."

Lumper intercedes, "Now, does he have to lick the compartments or can he clean it out with his finger and lick that?"

"No," my brother announces, "He will put his tongue in the actual compartment itself."

Lumper is in for five. Jay McBroom wants to know if the kid has to finish all the cheese that remains.

"No," says my brother, "one lick."

Jay McBroom adds his five to the growing pile. A gentleman behind us explains he couldn't help overhearing our wager and wonders if he can get a piece of the action.

"Of course," says my brother.

His companion considers himself an expert on human nature.

"That young man was raised too well. Simply look at his attire. You have it all wrong to believe he would stoop to such crassness."

His theory is heartily met with, "Put your money where your mouth is, Pal."

"Okay, but can he use his finger to . . ."

"No."

"Alright, I'm in."

And so is the gentleman next to him. Then, like a fire at the gauze works, one can see the bet spread through the stands. It travels up and over the portals, around pillars, over to the next section, and to the next. The ushers sense something is amiss. They alertly employ a walkie-talkie and request back up. More ushers arrive and take their stations. Too late, the betting continues to spread. High above us and to the right I can see a man take out his money, point to the kid, then mime the licking of the compartment to this neighbor. The neighbor reaches into his pocket. Somewhere across the field a section cheers. We all lean in fast and look at the kid. Was it a premature lick? No, it was only the Twins scoring the go-ahead run. We are led to understand it was a terrific play. Someone starts to explain it.

"Shut up."

For we have arrived at the moment of truth. The unsuspecting child has finished his last nacho. There is not a peep. I can hear a cricket in the bleachers as everyone leans in, all eyes focused on the nacho container and the child of destiny.

"Come on," a man blurts.

"Shhhhh, you'll spook him."

I hear whispering, "Lick it."

"Don't lick it."

"Lick it."

"Don't lick it."

"For god's sake, lick it."

"Come on, lick it you little . . ."

"Come on, come on, please, oh please."

"Shut up."

"You shut up."

The kid looks left, and then he looks right. And as the child of fortune tongues that cheese compartment, a cheer erupts the likes of which I'd never heard before or since at the dome. The entire outfield section began yelling as one, loud, raucous, and insane. The members of both baseball squads turn and face our party, our party that is now in a destructive frenzy and under assault by a goon squad of heavily armed ushers. We will pay heavily for this outburst, but for that brief moment in time the Minnesota Twins are watching us. It is the ecstasy. Then, as God is my witness, Kirby Puckett, center fielder and future member of the National Baseball Hall of Fame, smiles at our merry band and doffs his cap.

The Coldest Game

STEVE MARSH

An entire generation of Vikings fans grew up in a bubble. Sheltered by the Teflon skies of the Metrodome, our parents subjected us to endless humblebraggadocio about the "frigid tundra" of Met Stadium in the 1970s. Snowmobile suits and schnapps and Coach Bud Grant barring sideline space heaters. We grew up feeling like we had missed out on something cooler than cool.

That is until 2015, the second of two interim seasons that the Vikes played on the University of Minnesota campus at TCF Bank Stadium, while construction continued on US Bank Stadium. The team won the NFC North, ensuring an outdoor playoff game in Minnesota for the first time since 1976.

The Vikings drew the Seahawks, a squad only a couple of seasons removed from Super Bowl success, and with a famous "Twelfth man" fan base. Welcome to Minneapolis, you one-clicking, venti-latte-with-soy–soaked fish tossers!

Early in the week, the forecast called for a cold game, but nothing historic: zero degrees or one below. By Wednesday, those numbers started to plummet, and now it looked like we would be taking our place in the history books. In the newspaper, weatherman Paul Douglas described "a Thelma and Louise temperature trend"—that is, a drop "off the cliff."

I remember looking around social media that week and feeling that I wasn't alone in my perversion: We all wanted to suffer, the Domed generation especially. And we wanted to subject Seattle and its fans to hostile weather that we would revel in.

That being said, despite all the sadomasochistic forecast-peeping, it was surprisingly hard to find somebody to take my other ticket. Finally, my boy Andy, who grew up in Florida, declared he was down. He's a motorcycle guy and a bit of an adrenaline junkie, but he isn't stupid. He began looking for a parka upgrade and warm boots. My dad suggested bringing cardboard to protect our feet from the frozen concrete. (Dad has hobo skills?) I actually scavenged for some boxes, but as my Uber pulled away from the apartment at 8:30 a.m., I realized I'd left them on the kitchen table.

I met Andy outside TCF at 9:00 a.m. The skies looked clear blue and the air temperature registered at a hyperborean nine degrees below zero.

The kind of air that hurts your gums when you breathe. Across the TCF parking lots, Vikings fans behaved like wildlings beyond the wall: tossing footballs, grilling meats, passing around jugs of fermented fluid that could double as windshield de-icer. My tailgating cousins had prepped a big pot of chili and we hung out in their butane-heated tent for a couple of hours.

By kickoff, the temp had climbed to six degrees below zero with a twenty-five below zero windchill. That made it the coldest game in Vikings history (take that, Dad!), and the third-coldest game ever, trailing only a fluky nine-degree game in Cincinnati (1982) and the legendary Ice Bowl in Green Bay (1967). It was so cold that the Gjallarhorn (ba-BAAAAA! ba-BAAAAAAA!) shattered before kickoff and needed to be replaced with an older model from storage. It wasn't cold enough to prevent then-eighty-eight-year-old Bud Grant from running on to the field for the coin toss in shirtsleeves. Kinky.

Of course the game played out as a tightly contested, teeth-clattering affair. The Vikings executed three hard-earned field goals, and at six degrees below zero, a 9-0 lead seemed insurmountable. But they allowed the Seahawks back into the game on one of those are-you-kidding-me broken plays by Russell Wilson, and gave them the lead after a fumble by Adrian Peterson.

My buddy Andy spent most of the third quarter huddling in a concourse bathroom trying to get feeling back into his feet. It didn't seem right Andy should lose his toes for nothing, though, and sure enough, by the time he returned, Teddy Bridgewater was calmly driving us toward the win on a two-minute drill. With twenty-six seconds remaining, and the Vikes down by one, Blair Walsh lined up a twenty-seven-yard field goal. I remember the guy in front of me turned his back toward the field, locked eyes with me, and said, "I can't look."

When Blair missed—of course he missed—the entire stadium fell silent. The ten-year-old boy standing next to me began to quietly cry. And then we shuffled out of the stadium—not wildlings now but wights.

At almost every major stage in my lifetime, the Vikings have broken my heart. I understand that being a fan of anything is a foolhardy proposition. The Internet has become our great engine of disillusionment: all our heroes are sexual deviants who are in it for the money. These days, it's naive to fan out on anybody, whether an actor or a politician or a musician, so why would a grown adult root for a professional sports franchise? Especially a professional franchise with a reputation for heartbreaking futility in the biggest possible moments? My purple psychological scars aren't as old as the first generation's, the scars caused by the hallowed patriarchy of Bud Grant, but they are old enough to drink. And we all know that insanity is doing the same thing over and over again and expecting different results.

And I have a feeling, a literal feeling, that the pain from this one, from the loss of the coldest game, will last longer than the mental and spiritual disappointment from all those past seasons. They say that in the aftermath of bad frostbite you never stop feeling shards of glass in the affected area, like real-life stigmata or something. I remember my first football coach used to say terrible weather always feels better when you win. Well, we lost again. And this time, that loss will be written upon our extremities forever.

Elegy for the Metrodome

MATT RASMUSSEN

An outdoors that is somehow indoors.—David Berman

You always held your breath
while we were failing

and even those rare moments
we weren't. Dear fiberglass

cavern that held us like a giant
yet soft mouth, I first

became a cell in your bowl
of bodies. Your blue seats

bloomed in tiers, each one
unfolding an embrace held

open by our weight.
As a boy, I would lie in bed

and behold your pressurized
darkness. How could something

be so empty and so about to burst?
It became a seated thought

in the stadium of my skull.
If you think about it,

there was no outdoors
before there was an indoors.

Within your symmetry
we only felt more imperfect.

If I am inside something
then there must be something

within me. Who will weep
for the lost indoors of America?

Where are our indoorsmen
willing to chain themselves

to an escalator? Because air
held you up, your collapse could

never stop arriving. Would our breath
have kept your roof aloft?

From afar you looked like someone
strapped down a cloud

or built a giant pillow
for the sky. But why?

Are there doors we don't know
we're inside? You will never

swallow us again never
let us touch our knee to your never

thirsty lawn and no one now will ever
raise a finger toward your Teflon sky.

O giant lung, exhale me home.

The Mauer Myth

ROBERT O'CONNELL

If it were possible to collect the motions that make up high-level professional sports and preserve them in a museum, the left-handed swing of the Minnesota Twins' Joe Mauer, in his prime, would need a place. His was the kind that seemed not only useful but definitional; baseball fans could watch it and sense the game clarified.

The dogged statistician might have asked for more power, trading some singles for home runs. The efficiency expert could point out that his carefulness at the plate, his preference for walking versus chasing a bad pitch, had the effect of tamping his aggression. But the aesthete had no such qualms. From a textbook posture—his frame tall and relaxed, his legs slightly horseshoed, the bat eddying behind his ear—Mauer charted the very concept of hitting in all its permutations. He caught up to fastballs and waited on curves. He pulled his hands in or cast the barrel out. He had an eye for every pitch and access to the full range of corresponding outcomes: the hair's-width take for ball four, the rolling single over second base, the line drive touching down in a gap, the odd homer over whichever section of the outfield wall. Batters could fill encyclopedias with the frustrations of their trade, their accounts of "fighting it," but Mauer's approach evinced a different kind of relationship, a full and fundamentally appreciative commitment.

Not many athletes have ever lived better—or seemed to, as much as such a thing can be gleaned from newspapers, TV interviews, and the general ballpark mood—than the young, St. Paul-bred Mauer. He debuted with the Twins as a twenty-year-old rookie and entrenched himself as baseball's best catcher for the better part of the next decade. At the plate, he was the essential piece of the lineup for a perennial playoff contender. Behind it, he had a sharp mind for pitch sequencing and a strong, accurate arm. He had starred in football, basketball, and baseball at Cretin-Derham Hall High School, some eight miles from downtown Minneapolis, before the Twins made him the first overall selection in the 2001 draft. The hometown-kid-makes-good angle might have been schmaltzy were it not so richly detailed. Mauer really did have the kind of frame that seemed shaped by farm work: tall and broad, inclined toward practicality, under close-cropped hair and a valedictorian's smile. His chief virtue as a ballplayer really was his patience; his chief virtue as a public figure really was his politeness. Plenty of athletes might have said, as Mauer once did, "I really haven't even thought about playing anywhere but here." Few could have given the impression that they actually meant it.

***

One evening in 2013, in a game against the New York Mets, that chapter of Mauer's life ended. A seventh-inning foul tip hammered off of his catcher's mask, and though he stayed in to finish the game, he was later diagnosed with a concussion. The immediate symptoms gave way to lingering ones, headaches and vision issues. Mauer missed the remainder of the season.

When he returned the next year, it was as a different player. Instead of catching, he played first base. He went hitless his first day back and again the next, setting off on the least distinguished year of his baseball life. He batted a career-low .277 and dropped out of consideration altogether for the Silver Slugger and Gold Glove, awards that had once been his as a matter of course. The seasons that followed were even worse: .265, then .261. Mauer had once described hitting as, "You see the ball coming in, and everything is nice and easy, and you put a good swing on it." Now he tracked pitches through a fog.

The terror of watching a once-great athlete diminish is that so much of it is invisible. Mauer looked much the same as he used to, standing at the plate, and when he sent a single hard the other way, it would seem for a second that he had snapped himself back into place. But the broader results, the weak groundouts and winnowing averages, said otherwise. Whatever misalignment the concussion had caused announced itself daily as the most basic kind of entropy. Things simply didn't work out well as often as they used to.

His folk-heroic status made it harder. Minneapolis is not immune to the cruelties of the sports town, and there were plenty of calls for the Twins to bench Mauer or trade him, and rampant griping about his contract. Sadder yet were the supportive sounds inside the stadium: the over-hopeful chatter when his spot in the order would come up, followed by the silent sigh—so as not to offend—when he struck out. Worst of all was the disproportionate applause when he managed to guide a ball out of the infield. An overwhelming feeling of obligation hung in the ballpark. Mauer had played so well, and in a manner that so reflected how his community liked to imagine itself, that his downturn became an occasion for reimbursement. It was time for Twins fans to show they had deserved him, and that was exactly as glum as it sounds.

On the rare occasions that Mauer talked about his struggles, he did so in temporary terms. "I'm trying to do everything I can to get back," he told the *Pioneer Press*. "It just takes time." He spoke the way players have always spoken about slumps, even once it becomes obvious to everyone else that what is being called a slump has become routine.

***

And then, 2017. It would be too neat to suggest that Mauer willed himself to his former powers. It was not a magical year, and when it comes time for the full telling of his career, it will hardly register. But given what came before—the almost flawless decade, the foul tip, the sudden and then lasting swoon—it was clarifying. Mauer made the cliché true: he showed what he was made of.

The Twins, who had lost 103 games the year prior, went 85-77 and snuck into the postseason as a wild card team. They got the sort of scattered, unpredictable, and not-to-be-repeated contributions that those sorts of teams need. Byron Buxton, their promising young centerfielder, started spraying triples to go along with his daredevil defense. Miguel Sano, the mountain of a third baseman, hit the ball hard, when he hit it. The thirty-year-old second baseman Brian Dozier suddenly came into possession of pure home run power.

Although Mauer was better than he had been in years, hitting .305 and driving in seventy-one runs, a given night's key plays were likely to come from elsewhere on the roster. But there was one way in which this new Mauer improved on the original one. The connotations that he had carried so well in his youth—the all-that-is-right-about-Minnesota stuff—took on a new and profound resonance.

Before, he had been an uncannily realized ideal, the provincial self-regard tidily packaged up and winning batting titles. Now, he expanded to actually embody what he had previously just suggested, about selflessness and gumption and hard work. He had labored to become just a portion of what he once was; he applied that portion as best he could. The younger Mauer had seemed like he *would* do these things, but he'd also seemed like he would never need to.

For the first time in a while, Mauer was a reliable contributor. But more, he seemed to exert a kind of hopeful, sub-statistical influence on the team, by dint of who he was and how he played. A Mauer hit—a hard shot up the middle or a vintage inside-out slice to deep left—still had the feeling of a commencement, of outlining the scope of baseball's possible things. The big eighth-inning runs felt strangely foretold by his third-inning singles.

The talk around Minneapolis that summer didn't often center on Mauer; the younger players were both more important and more plainly exciting, the real engines of the surprise run. But the relative quiet seemed like its own kind of reward, one tailored to its recipient. His swing was still pretty. His story again fit.

Cycling Season

WILLIAM SOUDER

It's August and I am on my bike. That's true most of the time in warm weather, but it is true almost every day in August, the richest month and the most heartbreaking. A bike is a good place to see August from. I wouldn't miss it.

Minneapolis is more bike-obsessed by the year, and its bike paths will take you places—but not everywhere I want to go. My destinations are not points on a map. They're states of mind. Every serious cyclist eventually needs more, and arrives here, beyond the edge of the city in bike country. Out here, long pelotons of cyclists sweep along the wide shoulders of the county highways every evening, and individual riders pick their way through the casual bikers exploring the paved trails that tunnel through the woods between the city and the St. Croix River. I have been biking since before Lemond wore the yellow jersey and the term "bike friendly" was applied to places that are not that. Sharing the road with cars is a fraught enterprise. I can do it, but I'd truly rather not.

I like to ride alone, keeping my own tempo. But I ride hard. My bike is a fancy one, close cousin to the bikes they race in the Tour de France and proof that your toys get more expensive as you get older. It's a wonderful machine, feather-light and nimble. When you push it, the bike leaps forward and the tires emit a rhythmic hiss against the pavement—*swoosh swoosh swoosh*—with each pedal stroke. Every hard turn of the cranks is a thrill.

I am passed from time to time, usually by riders half my age. But my demographic is well-represented out on the road, too, and a few of them are astonishingly fast. You can spot them. A fringe of gray beneath the helmet, the muscled legs that are strong but not young. Knowing where they've been, they know where they're going. They like a good pace.

Summers wander in unpredictably in this northern place, but by August the season is in full possession of Minnesota. The air is sultry, the fields and forests lush. The season hangs motionless, yet it carries hints of things to come. The birds, passions spent and nests emptied, have gone silent. Ducks and geese are finishing their molts and taking to the air with their young to rehearse for the journey south that lies ahead. The angle of the sun is changing. The farmers' markets groan with the harvests. Before the month is out, clouds of blackbirds will swim across the sky and the warm days will melt into cool evenings. I'll ride on into September and October, maybe even get out once or twice in the Indian Summer of November, though it is a sad business to ride in those brown and barren days.

Of course, you see a lot from a bike. Last summer I went out one afternoon just after a line of storms had passed, and followed the rain clouds as they headed east. The pavement was wet and steaming. The air was thick. A few miles from home the sky darkened. The storm turned back on itself and came straight at me just as the road turned broadside to it. In seconds I was submerged in a blinding deluge. The wind was tremendous and I had to lean into it to stay upright. Pellets of hail bounced off the roadway. It was glorious. I didn't want it to stop, and I felt a pang for those unappreciative mortals who will never plunge into the murk on two wheels. But it did stop. The sun came out, the wind shifted, and I watched as the storm, which seemed to have made a special detour for my benefit, rushed off to another place.

These days I like the idea of trying to outride the end of summer, though I know it's not possible. Here is what I see on my way: the arc of County Road 7 bending steeply down toward Sunset Lake, where I can descend at more than thirty miles an hour. The farm where they keep two burros. Someone mowing the grass in the small cemetery near the Withrow Ballroom. Emerald oceans of corn and soybeans. Wetlands choked with cattails. A big cattle operation that reminds me of South Dakota, and where the yawning door and loft windows of a barn look like the features of a startled human face. The bridge over Highway 96 on the Gateway Trail where you have to go around the horse droppings, and a little further on, the pasture with the open gate that marks the place where the trail begins to drop and riding feels suddenly headlong and effortless as the forest blurs on either side of you. Windrows of hay, open fields, immense horizons. This huge, beautiful world of ours.

This particular summer happens to be the one in which the government says I have reached "full retirement age." This information seems unconnected to my actual life. I am not retired. As long as I have my wits about me, I won't be retiring. Too many things to see, places to go, books to write. Too many roads to ride.

And so I am on my bike. A long hill looms ahead. There is so much to take in that it is hard to be alone with my thoughts. Near the crest an oak towers over the roadway. The late afternoon sun threads though its canopy, casting a filigree of shadow across the lane. I let myself imagine that each leaf is marking the place where it will fall in October. Everything has its season and all good things must end, except for these perfect moments, which are eternal. I have miles to go. Days. Years.

The road rises. My legs ache and my lungs are heaving. I'll be home soon, ready to ride another day. It's August. I am on my bike. I lean forward, come off the saddle, and stand on the cranks.

The Secret Handshake

MAX ROSS

When my car's battery died on a bitterly cold January day, my father refused to come to my apartment in south Minneapolis to give me a jump.

He drives a Tesla and claimed (not quite accurately) that using it to power a regular car would cause it to short-circuit. "Plus, it's nasty outside," he said, "and, as you know, your father is a wuss."

Luckily my stepfather, Kevin, agreed to help. He is bald, clean-shaven, slender, friendly, and handy. An agricultural engineer, he has a master's degree in weed science and subscribes to journals such as *Wheat Life*. He always knows what time it is. "I'll be there in fifteen minutes," he said. He arrived at my apartment in fifteen minutes.

I thought this would be my chance, finally, to impress him. The winter before, I had called him in distress when my car had blown a tire. I didn't know how to change it, and he had to do it for me, kneeling in the cold on the side of a busy street.

He had also, at various points, fixed leaks in my kitchen and helped me assemble (that is, he assembled) a desk from Ikea. Around him I felt inept, and although we are polite to each other (kind, even), my sense is that he views me as his wife's hapless son, part of the bargain of marrying her.

I did know how to jump a car, however, and now made a demonstration of setting the cables in place. "The red clamp's on the positive terminal," I said with authority.

Kevin fixed the corresponding clamps to his truck's battery and said, "Let's give it a go."

I prayed that the jump would work and that my competence would be established evermore. Outside my window, Kevin gave a rather solemn thumbs-up.

I turned the key. The engine sputtered, didn't engage. I tried again. Nothing.

"Looks like you'll need a new battery," Kevin said.

He and my mother met seven years ago through a dating service called It's Just Lunch. They discovered common interests in hiking and wine. They went on trips to vineyards, first in rural Minnesota, then to

Napa Valley and the Oregon coast. On their hikes, they wore clothes with many pockets and zippers. In the evenings, they visited wineries. Within a year, they were engaged.

I was relieved when they married. My mother had spent the previous several years in a muddle. A decade before, without warning, my father had informed her that he was gay, and their marriage dissolved. The future she had expected (simply, to be with him) also dissolved. In its place was nothing.

I was sixteen at the time, and for my last two years of high school, we lived alone. For her, it was an era of bathrobes, insomnia, Sleepytime tea, Kleenex, rationalization ("everything happens for a reason"), reheated leftovers, and worry.

Kevin appeared as a steady arm.

My relationship with him has evolved slowly and sometimes awkwardly. We're members of the same gym and sometimes see each other in the locker room. If we're both naked, we make a point of speaking, as if doing so will shield us from the mild embarrassment of our nudity, from the Oedipal drama once removed. Our talk is stilted, crisp: "Hey! How are you?" "Good." "Good!" "Okay. Good to see you." "Yes!" (Exclamations are mine.) But in truth, this is how we always are. If we're out to dinner or happen to meet in the grocery store, we still act as if we're naked in the locker room.

Now, I wondered how we might get my car to a repair shop to have the battery replaced. Kevin made it known we would be changing it ourselves.

From the back of his truck he took out his toolbox. "Yup, it's always with me," he said. The heads of wrenches and screwdrivers shone inside as if they had never been used. No, it was as if they had been used often but cleaned extremely well.

We took off our gloves and set to work. The temperature was below zero. Snot froze in our noses. Our breath huffed up above us.

Kevin loosened the bolts that held the battery in place. So we wouldn't lose them, I placed the nuts in a ceramic coffee mug that had been in my car. This was my job, to hold the mug. Our hands quickly became achy with numbness. When Kevin could no longer feel his fingers, he suggested we warm up in his truck.

The truck's interior, like Kevin's toolbox, was spotless. In the years he'd owned it, he had made zero imprint upon the inside of the truck. But then I thought: No, tidiness was his mark. He is an orderly man and maintains his truck to his fullest expression. The radio was tuned to the Vikings-Seahawks playoff game. Teddy Bridgewater threw an incomplete pass. The Vikings, as ever, punted.

"Not looking good," I said. "I mean, not sounding good. Ha."

"Nope," Kevin said.

Thus, our conversation reached its terminus.

My phone buzzed in my pocket—my father. His message said: "Picture's ready. Plz pick up."

We had recently spent two hours in a picture frame shop consulting each other on how best to frame an illustration of a Dutch trade ship. ("See, Son, you don't want the frame to overpower the picture. And the backing should have a little color to it, but again, you don't want it to overwhelm.")

My father and I could have a picture framed artfully, but we couldn't replace a car battery. If left to our own devices, those devices would break and would stay broken until we paid people to fix them. My inheritance was a moderate streak of dandyism and a set of deficient motor skills. As I typed him a reminder that I was momentarily without transportation, my phone's screen went black. Its battery, too, had died.

The battery store, a rectangular building with a pair of chimneys on top, resembled a battery. When my eyeglasses defogged, I saw batteries of all sizes gleaming on the shelves. I carried my dead battery in my hands, feeling a little silly about it, as if I were taking my own half-eaten croissant into a pastry shop.

The Vikings game was on the radio there, too. Six clerks stood around a counter, looking upward toward a ceiling speaker. One of them mentioned how many rushing yards the Vikings' running back had accumulated during the season. Another mentioned how many he had two years ago. A third added how close he was to breaking the season record.

They were playing a game of their own, as men often do: a game of information, to see who knew the most. Eventually one of the clerks saw us and approached.

I explained, holding my dead battery, that I needed a new battery. The clerk led us to a shelf and showed us three that looked the same. He explained how they weren't. All I understood was that their prices were different. Kevin suggested I get the second-cheapest one—just as I would have done, applying the wine theory I use in restaurants.

As I paid, the Vikings missed a field goal that would have won the game, so they lost. Many knowledgeable Minnesotans had predicted this, and in predicting it had secretly hoped it would happen, which made the loss, in a backward way, a win. The clerk looked up at the speaker. "Just like '98," he said.

"The Atlanta Falcons," Kevin said. "Gary Anderson."

"First field goal he missed all year."

I understood the game's rules but couldn't participate. I was a spectator of my gender.

As we installed the new battery, the dynamic between Kevin and me didn't shift. I stood beside him, holding the mug of nuts and screws. Now and then he pointed, directing me to shine a flashlight under the hood. He worked quickly, seldom speaking. He spoke so little, in fact, that he never spoke. But our quiet was relaxed; we were united by our task.

When Kevin's fingers went numb, he handed me the wrench. Without a word, he nodded his head. My hands were cold as well, nearly useless. But I saw it was important to him that I finish the work on my own car. My brain told my fist to close around the wrench and not let go, lest my incompetence reveal itself. Soon the new battery was in place.

I stepped into my car. Outside my window, Kevin gave a rather solemn thumbs-up. He didn't smile when the engine started, but by not smiling, he did.

"You're all set," he said.

We removed our gloves and shook hands. Our hands were chilly and blocky, but we had put them to good use. Through them, we had communed and communicated. And our handshake, I sensed, had completed our conversation in the secret language of male intimacy, a language in which I am still struggling to gain fluency.

Minneapolis, revisited

SHANNON GIBNEY

They said the city was a testament to liberal pragmatism. They said that the gaunt-eyed brown children of the borderless had ruined it. And their vacant, earnest parents, always wanting more.

Let too many in, they will multiply. Overstay their welcome.

A park a seven-mile walk from each and every citizen. A giant polar bear bike propelled by fifteen cyclists racing through the neighborhood pursued by gangs of four-year-olds who *just want to touch it.* A po-mo theater with a modernist message. And taiko drumming on Thursdays.

Wintertime half the year well-spent *if you use it to make art. And nooky.* Shanties on frozen waterways, with karaoke and coloring books. Lake of the Isles on your lips every spring or summer afternoon, arm hooked through your best friend's or your lover's. Autumn almost gone already.

And one day, a man driving with his girlfriend and her daughter pulled over by the police; shot while complying with their request. One day a friend, a son, a brother, the next day nothing. And the next day and the next day and the next day and the next the city eats itself, until it finally produces something which calms us: DISRUPTION. DISRUPTION.
Shut. It. Down.
Withered white hands, wringing.
Our brown ones flinging.

*

Bikes and bike lanes and greenways and pedestrian-bike walkways and bridges.
The heft and weight of the wind in your palm when you step outside on April mornings. The sweetness of dandelions.

The strange relationship between the person you wanted to be when you moved here and the person you are now. Suburbanites moving into your neighborhood, the same place you moved years ago. Your anger, and your abiding happiness. A community garden on every corner.

The reasons why you stay.

Everything that has come before.

The Mississippi.

The money. The pain. The pain of the money.
When we said, "Minnesota Miracle," we didn't mean yours. We didn't mean you.

Minneapolis:

How many homes can you dare to encompass without the panacea of *progress*?

What courthouses, police precincts, schools, storefronts, stoops will our footfalls take us to if we walk on without asking?

Will the parks still shine if they are burning?

And how much of you is us, now that we have claimed you?

You Tell Me

SOFIA BURFORD

In the Twin Cities, I am considered Hispanic, since I was born in Mexico and later emigrated to the US. But I have never imposed the "Hispanic" adjective on myself. It just happens to be one of the labels I was given here.

I lived in Minneapolis in 1994 for a brief period, then moved back to Mexico, where I lived for ten years. In 2006, I returned to the US, living in Kansas City first, and then moving to the Twin Cities in 2012, where I continue to live today. I was born a Mexican citizen in 1960, and I could not be more Mexican. My grandmother's brother was the leader of the Mexican Revolution in 1910, elected President in 1911, and assassinated in 1913. You can find him on a mural at Boca Chica restaurant in West St. Paul.

I married my husband thirty years ago in Mexico. He is an American citizen, born in Texas, but who grew up in Mexico City. Today, I am an American citizen. After having lived in the US for many years with a green card, I am proud to say that I was naturalized as a US citizen in St. Paul in 2017. As the US Federal Building is only a few blocks away from where I live, I walked, with both apprehension and joy, to my naturalization ceremony on a sunny day. I now hold both Mexican and American citizenships.

I find it easier to live here today because the Hispanic population in this area has grown significantly and I am not as alone when facing some of the trials and tribulations related to living in this country as a minority. Also, technology advancements today permit me to remain connected to my friends and family in Mexico. So I have a much stronger support system. On a practical note, I love the fact that it is now possible to buy Mexican avocados year-round in most local grocery stores.

And yet, I also find it harder to live here, because there are mobs that don't know what to make of minorities in this country. And minorities are now, perhaps more than ever before, a constant subject of conversation. The media seems to bombard the general public with divisive messages. I am tired of hearing about problems related to Hispanics, Mexicans, illegals, DACAs, or refugees. Even US-born Americans with Spanish last names cannot be safe from this storm. Press coverage shows people advocating that some minorities should not be here, that they should just pack up and go home. If we are living in the land where it is a universal right to pursue happiness, why is it that some think they are the only ones entitled to this right?

Every day I am constantly reminded that I am a minority. I go to the doctor and I'm asked if I'm Hispanic. The dentist also wants to know, as if this would make my teeth different. I take a writing class and they ask me. I get a job and I'm asked once again. I set up an Internet account, and they also want to know. Everybody wants to know.

Why is this relevant?

Today, I walk around at the Mall of America and I am no longer surprised to hear someone speaking Spanish. Twenty-five years ago, if I had heard someone speaking Spanish, I would have approached them and asked, "Hey, where are you from? When did you come here? What brought you here?" Today, I know I cannot do that. It is taboo. People resent it if I dare to spring those questions on them. People are fearful and question my intentions. "Are you from immigration?" I was once asked. I apologized for wanting to connect.

Strange laws govern us these days. We must mind our own business and try to stay out of others' ways. But, oh, how I wish I could connect with, and embrace, many strangers that surround me, especially those who might relate to my story. I am still seen as an "other," an "alien," and as someone once told me, "from another race." I have often wondered from what other race I could be? I have been categorized as a "person of color." I am Mexican, yet my skin is delicate and full of freckles. I need to hide from the sun. Very often, when people meet me, they will say, "You don't look Mexican."

What is Mexican supposed to look like?

Now I am a naturalized citizen, placed in the category of Hispanic. And yet I am still the same old me, oftentimes just struggling with life's daily challenges like everybody else. So many adjectives to describe me: Mexican, Mestiza, Mexican Indian, Spaniard, Sephardic Jew, converted Catholic, French, non-resident alien, resident alien, American or US citizen, foreign national, naturalized citizen. All this, in addition to Hispanic, Latina, and woman of color.

"What am I?" I ask.

Why don't you tell me, since you seem to know?

People here still like to talk about the weather and sports all the time. Some local TV stations still have the same weather forecasters, albeit looking a quarter century older. I am sure I do, too. The lakes still freeze and winters are still very long. It snows in mid-April. I'm wearing the same jacket I bought in Minneapolis twenty-five years ago. Yet when people find out that I am originally from Mexico, they still ask me the same question: "What is your favorite Mexican restaurant here?"

And I know they don't like the answer I usually give them: "I don't have one, as I really prefer to cook my Mexican meals at home." People now dare to ask me: "Are you a citizen?" As my late mother-in-law used to like to say, as she rolled her eyes: *"Que más da?"* "What difference does it make?"

The most significant change I see with living in the Twin Cities today is in my own life. The first time I lived here, my children were two and four years old. There was not much I could do on my own, as I spent my days and nights looking after them. Now that they are grown, and have moved on to live their own lives, it is much easier to enjoy the beautiful bike trails and the wonderful library that I have a few blocks away from home. The cultural opportunities as well as the classical music concerts enrich my life. I love living here today, even when I'm considered an outsider.

I often wonder what the Twin Cities will be like in another twenty-five years. But if I'm being honest, I'm not in a hurry to find out.

Minneapolis Public

DAVID MURA

There are 150 first languages in our schools
and so many aliens even E.T. would go unnoticed,
though if your tongue moved one way in the land of your birth
it must move another now, awkward at first.

There are blacks here who've never been to Africa;
Africans who've never heard a Baptist prayer,
much less the solemn dirges of Lutherans
or how the artist formerly known is some sort of Prince.

In the anthology of American Buddhist poetry
you will find not one face of a Tibetan
but they are here with girls and boys named Tenzin
and one, my son's good friend, throws a hard mean spiral.

Esmir is not the name of a girl but a Bosnian
boy who crouches at a table and glues a lamp together
and later with my other son conspires on a book—*A Touch
of Rabies*—a heartbreaking tale of good dogs gone bad.

(Why tell a soul of the sieges that brought him here
or stories of the Dalai Lama or the temples destroyed
or troops of the warlords in the streets of Somalia,
the borders dividing death from safety if not evil and good?)

Say you're Egyptian or Haitian: Here you're singular,
not part of a Big Apple ghetto. If you're Chinese,
most likely you're adopted, or else your parents study
engineering at the U. And have I mentioned the Mexicans?

In *West Side Story* the rumble starts with Puerto Ricans
and working-class whites in a high school gym;
this year Maria's still Natalie Wood white to Jamaica's
half-black Anita, and the Jets sport blacks, one Tibetan,

and my happa daughter who still doesn't question
such casting, or why *Bye Bye Birdie* last year
just might not be the choice of half the school
for a song and dance they could take on as their own.

Still at the spring school dance J-Lo and Ja Rule
set the awkward bump and grind of junior high girls
and the boys watch on the sidelines as boys that age do,
whether Bosnian, black, white, Somali, Tibetan.

I'm told we live in the Land of Great Lake Wobegon
where all the women are strong, the men good looking,
and the children above average—and, I always add,
everyone's white. Hey, Tenzin, Nabil, go tell Garrison:

Not now. Not quite.

Parkway Theater, 1969

SHEILA O'CONNOR

Nights we entered through the exit, petty criminals with stolen Newports in our pockets, the flicker of forbidden films flashing on the screen. Every movie we saw was rated R. Inside the dark, the smell of buttered popcorn mixed with sweat, snow on strangers' skin, wet coats, and cigarettes. The suck of sticky floor beneath our boots. So little of what we saw we understood, or we understood only as shadows.

Bored, we climbed the stairs up to the bathroom, drawn by the opulence of red walls flocked in white and the silvered ornate mirror above the sink. Lost wealth, that much we understood. Everything about the place was fallen. Later, the Parkway had a long run showing porn. But even before we'd stepped into thirteen, that theater was sex. Or what we believed was sex. The sagging, nubby seats. The solo men tucked back in corners.

Winter nights, we stayed through double features, feasted off abandoned bags of popcorn, boxes of Junior Mints and Milk Duds we scavenged off the floor. And up there on the screen, Dunaway and Beatty ran reckless from the law. A pair we longed to be. My Clyde to her brave Bonnie. Bonnie that I loved. Freckle-faced and brilliant in her own maroon beret. My Bonnie who read *Poor Richard's Almanac*, and named her German shepherd Socrates. My Bonnie, who ended up in prison. Prostitution. Drugs. Burglary. Police reports appearing in the paper. A girl entering through exits. A girl that night with her hands over her face, afraid to watch our heroes slaughtered in a bloodbath.

"Let's go," she said, and for the first time we walked out through the lobby. Stepped through the dirty glass doors into winter, into snow glittering like silver in the glow of the marquee. The fear of death behind us. The fear of life ahead.

Powderhorn

ED BOK LEE

Cowbell wind chimes clang
In this quiet pocket of the city.

Lesbians love living here.
Brutalized philosophers

Of color. Pit bull walkers. Exiles.
Immigrants. Jugglers. Where

Grizzly hippies spill coffee
Over the Crisis of Capitalism,

Apiary priests pray to their bees, and hydra-
Headed emcees slowly go gray.

Kingdom of nightshade, weeping
Willow, and concrete. City

Lake cosmos of nighttime
Stars wheeling a young

Boy's trowel in a front yard carrot patch
Sunday mornings beside tattoo-faced parents

On their hands and knees, weeding.
Toddler to the knowledge

That the world redesigned by yet another
Solar system in another galaxy begins

With each Glock's shot in the distance. Sirens
Sing their far syllables of sin and lament. Crack, smack, and sex

Workers shuffling subzero steps at the perimeter like puff-
Hooded sentinels, all winter into spring's

Newest chicks, pecking, clucking
Through broken vodka bottles and dandelions.

Midwest, Midtown
Contiguity of the future and past;

Part metropolis,
Part grassland.

Sunday futbol in Somali-slurred Spanish,
Pagan puppet street parade each May,

And Mike Hoyt's tri-ped portable karaoke
Projecting lyrics on a Greenway underpass

For punks, bankers, activists, nurses—anyone
On a summer Saturday night who brakes and croons

Before biking on. Meanwhile,
Lowriders shimmy. Native teens

In saggy pants glare or clown
By the monkey bars. Cops like orcas

Troll. And brothers brawl
With chain mail, ballet, and a basketball.

Once upon a time, the world longed
For milk, so the sun touched its aching tusks

To the moon's boiling door
To borrow a little soil, a little cloud,

Until old worms tunneled into new bones.
Meanwhile, the deer-dreaming wind spread seeds

And ashes over the earth. Snow
Soon joined in. Mulberry

Wine inside larks. All sky art. Pond-
Stewed ions. Humans. Meditation. Poetry. Shit,

I almost forgot—Chonny's Bhangra Basement Barbeque
Each Friday at sunset

For *anyone* who wants to get down
And churn

Their own color across this canvas.

The Long Road from Somalia

FATHIA ABSIE

When I was eight years old, I decided I was going to leave Somalia and come to the United States. By thirteen, I knew it was time. In Somalia, at that age you're considered an adult, because you can get married and have children and all that.

I did some research and I realized to get to the United states, I'd have to be an adult. So I put together this grand plan. I got a passport that made me twenty years old, then I got in touch with a friend of a friend of a friend who was studying in the United States, and she sent me a student visa.

I saved up some money. I also stole my mother's and grandmother's jewelry. Somalis like to wear a lot of gold jewelry. Then I went to Nairobi, Kenya, to sell it, which got me most of the money. But I was still short about 1,000 Kenyan shillings.

By chance, one of the people helping me ran into a famous Somali poet in Nairobi. He was in exile in Kenya, and my friend saw him in this restaurant and told him what was happening. He was from my sub-tribe. She didn't tell him my age, because he would have said, "Go back to your family." But he said, "Okay. I will donate the 1,000 shillings," and he gave her the money. Back in 1987, that probably could support a family for a whole month.

I bought myself a ticket and flew to America. When we landed at JFK, I went to the immigration officer and handed her my passport.

"Welcome to the USA," she said. Then she looked at my passport, and she kept looking and looking at it. Finally she said, "Well, you made it, but your visa expired eight hours ago. I'm afraid we're going to have to send you back to Somalia."

I started crying and crying and crying. I had these big tears rolling down my cheeks.

"Please stop crying," she said.

"You don't understand," I said. "This is where I belong! This is my country. I've always felt like this was my country. Please don't send me back!"

She took a moment, looked around, closed my passport and said, "Go! Just go, go, go!"

I ran so fast. I don't even know how I made it to my next flight to Washington, D.C. When I finally got there, I wanted to kiss the ground, but I thought that would be weird. So I started kissing the walls of the airport. Outside there were a bunch of cab drivers lined up. One of them came out of his cab.

"Are you okay?" he asked me.

"Never better!" I said.

"Do you need a ride?"

"I would love to, but where am I going to go?" I didn't have any idea, but somehow I knew everything was going to be okay.

"Where are you from?"

"Somalia."

"So am I," he said. "Let me make some phone calls." And he found this family that would take me in for the time being. From that moment, I was on my way. Every morning I would wake up and have these butterflies in my stomach, which I would find out is the feeling you get when you're in love.

The family that he took me to was very well-known. The father was from the same tribe as my mother, and I knew some of the family members from back home. So I stayed with them for about two weeks. I talked to other relatives in Washington, D.C., on my dad's side, and asked them if I could stay with them, but they didn't have a place for me. I had another relative who lived in New Orleans, and she said I could live with her. So she sent me a plane ticket and I went to New Orleans.

I stayed with her for about a year. But I wanted to become an actress and a singer. So I got my GED and I went to Los Angeles. When I first moved to LA, I lived with American families, and did light housekeeping and babysitting. Of course, they didn't know my real age. In Somalia, by the time you were my age, you can be married with children, so you carry yourself as older. I was the oldest child in my family so I was always very responsible.

LA was a crazy place. I don't know how I survived. I was even homeless once. In the beginning I stayed with different people, couch-jumping. But I had a car, and for a couple of weeks I lived in it. I would park by Brentwood or Beverly Hills, and the cops would never leave you alone. They would come to your window and say, "You gotta move along unless you live here." But it wasn't very long. Pretty soon I started a job, and eventually I was able to get a roommate.

I auditioned for a lot of things—music videos, TV shows. Back then people would look at me and say, "You look like you're from the Middle

East or from South America. You can't be African. You don't look African."
I had long, wavy hair. It was just before people found out where Somalia
is. Most people learned about Somalia after the civil war, from *Black Hawk
Down* and all that stuff.

As a young Muslim girl, I was on my own. When you want to get
into that business, people will feed you alcohol and drugs. Everybody
wants to get you into something that you don't want to do. I knew a lot of
young girls who got into drugs. I never sort of . . . it just never interested
me, but people were doing crazy stuff to realize their dreams. It was very
sad. Eventually I realized that it wasn't for me. I wasn't ready to sell my soul.

A few years later things went really bad in Somalia. Civil war broke
out. The government was ousted. Hundreds of thousands of people lost
their lives. Millions became refugees in neighboring countries, including
my family. In the meantime, those of us who were in the United States were
able to receive asylum, which gives you a green card. That let me sponsor
my family to come join me: ten of my siblings and both my parents. It was
just incredible. Here I was in the country that I loved so much, and now I
had my family. I felt whole.

But my family was in a different, dark place. They were depressed,
they had PTSD. They had witnessed so much pain. They had lost so many
people. They were falling apart. And I was working full-time, working so
hard trying to hold them together. I had all these responsibilities.

When my family first came to America, I brought them to Seattle,
because LA was very expensive. But they were going through a lot because
a lot of my siblings were young and inexperienced. My sister ran away
with this guy, got married, and had a baby. She got sick and passed away
within the first two years of being here. Then my father passed away. Other
siblings got in trouble a lot, so I decided to take what was left of my family
and leave Seattle.

In 2010, I moved to Minnesota because I wanted to pursue filmmak-
ing and storytelling. I thought it would be a good place because the largest
Somali population in the country is in Minneapolis. I thought it would be
a great place.

I lived in Eden Prairie and worked in downtown St. Paul for an organization called Echo, which made cultural outreach videos. I also did some
translation for the University of Minnesota. Echo was later bought by Twin
Cities Public Television.

As a single mom of two girls—one of them was not school age yet—I
had no childcare, so I worked from home a lot. But I didn't mind the drive

when I went into the office. I would go past the airport and up the Mississippi River. It was beautiful. Most people outside don't realize how beautiful Minnesota is. When I lived there, I did a lot of walking in nature. I love water, and there was water all around us. And while I was walking I started making these videos telling stories about American history and true stories about my life. Then I would put them on Facebook and YouTube and they would get a lot of views. That's how I started to build my following.

I'm kind of a loner. I went to the Somali mall a couple of times, but it's not my kind of place. I've lived in this country for so long, kind of on my own. I like a mixed environment where every shade of humanity is present. I don't feel excited just because everyone looks like me. If I wanted to be only with Somalis, I could have stayed in Somalia. But I didn't feel very welcome in Minnesota. And I felt that on both sides, not only with the Somalis, but with the Minnesotans of Scandinavian descent. It was hard to find a way to become part of a community.

In a way that was a mixed blessing. In those years I wrote a lot, I worked a lot, and I learned about the power of solitude. That's when I became good at my craft as a filmmaker and storyteller.

It was also a stressful time in the beginning. I noticed my hair thinning from the stress, so I decided to shave it off and wear a hijab to cover my bald head until it grew back. I never wore one before, but within a year I knew I would keep wearing it. I just loved the way I looked in it. It made me feel very safe, and comfortable, like I was being hugged all the time. But I also didn't feel like it separated me from everyone. Because if you love God, you love his creation, and you love all people. That's when I got more interested in reading the Koran and when I started to grow spiritually.

Minnesota is a beautiful place. There's a sense of calm. There's so much nature. The people are kind even if they're not always friendly. They might not want to be your friend, but they don't bother you. As an artist and a person, I grew a lot there. If I wouldn't have come to Minnesota, I wouldn't have accomplished all that I have.

Dakota Homecoming

GWEN NELL WESTERMAN

We are so honored that
   you are here, they said.
We know that this is
   your homeland, they said.
The admission price
   is five dollars, they said.
Here is your button
   for the event, they said.
It means so much to us that
   you are here, they said.
We want to write
   an apology letter, they said.
Tell us what to say.

Over There

SARAH STONICH

I did it for love. Crossed the border one city to the next—not any fraught border, no barbed wire—just the short haul from St. Paul to Minneapolis, though at the time Minneapolis did feel like another realm. Minneapolitans seemed *different,* as if their DNA clung to little Foshay-shaped towers, as if their hair was ruffled by a more westerly breeze. A terribly long time ago I'd lived among them in south Minneapolis, attending both West and Marshall University high schools and paying as much heed to the character of the city as any teen would—none. I dropped out of one school, then another, and moved back to my hometown of Duluth. Years later, more formed, I came back to land squarely in St. Paul.

Back when urban pioneers could buy neglected, drafty fixer-uppers cheaply, I tackled three historic houses on the same block—living in all with no intention of flipping them, though flipped they got, very, very slowly. I learned to strip woodwork and trick contractors into showing up for work and embraced the mindfulness of demolition. I got okay with sticking my hands blindly into walls packed with a century of filth to replace sash weights or eradicate bats dead and alive. My accessories included a respirator. Floating on particulates of fumes, I painted miles of woodwork with oil-based enamel (with a sand and tack between each coat). I became quite the stud-finder. The neighborhood was beautiful. I loved it. I stalked it—a leafy, quiet square mile of creaky, energy-inefficient Victorians choked with charm and plagued by squirrels. There were cobbled alleys and derelict duplexes. A perfect place to write. I lived yards from The Commodore, where F. Scott and Zelda famously debauched. A couple blocks away was a monthly poetry and prose salon at the University Club, hosted by literary maven Carol Connelly, the city's poet laureate—because St. Paul *has* one. I lived a few doors down from August Wilson and next door to an aspiring crime writer. After dusk, Garrison Keillor walked his red socks around the block, avoiding eye contact even then. A wannabe writers' paradise. A quirky place with great bars and a video store that stocked as many foreign films as blockbusters. I could wow non-native visitors with the weirdness of the Curling Club (yes, a broom) or steer them to the sidewalk fronting the Laurel Avenue rowhouses where the limestone sediment-pattern looks like a Japanese ink drawing titled *A Thousand Ardent Penises.*

Paul Wellstone's place was two streets over. He would greet my dog Ilsa as if she could vote and shook hands with diminutive constituents waiting for the school bus, including my then-kindergartner, Sam. But what really endeared me to him was our shared penchant for dumpster-diving (interesting things get pulled out of old houses in the throes of renovation) plus, for being a sane voice in D.C. (now known as the Nine Circles of Hell).

When a bookstore opened downstairs of the coffee shop where I wrote most mornings, I nearly passed out. Despite being beyond lapsed, I could drop in on the echo-filled St. Paul Cathedral for quiet time. There I heard a renowned English choir perform Barber's *Agnes Dei*—inarguably the saddest of all of songs, making me think, *when I die, play that,* Or worse, should I ever have to leave St. Paul, make it my exit music.

Growing a little smug about my neighborhood, I'd think à la Mike Meyers that if it's not St. Paul, it's crap. Then I met the guy. Our first date was at Frost's, where I'd been a love-it hate-it patron enduring a decade of uneven service and supper club fare. Admittedly, you can't beat the charm of the patio on an August night, nearly magical. It was an online date, and I was sick to death of those, so expectations were low. Normally I'd have met a date somewhere between, which in his case meant Midway, which meant no. He'd have to come to me, and if he complained about the drive just once . . .

Jon showed up smelling exactly right, looking like he'd stepped out of a Hugo Boss billboard, perfectly graying at the temples as if he might run for office. We married a year later, twenty feet from where we met, our party spilling out onto the patio one inky autumn night. After the honeymoon he went back to his house in NE Minneapolis, and I to mine in St. Paul. The following year, I moved in with him but the transition to his neighborhood was rough. Yes, there were two libraries, but one was in a strip mall. Not quite walking distance was an intersection with a cluster of shops, an old-world bakery, a decent-enough coffee shop, a little Shipping News weekly, and the gem of an old theater in dire need of restoration—an area thin on architecture and history save the streets named for presidents, so that way back in the aughts, new immigrants could learn them for their citizenship tests. The old pickle factories (four!) were long-gone. No charming little taverns or music venues, but Johnson Street had its own flock of turkeys which were a bane to drivers, amusing to the kids, and a thrill for dogs. I never took to the house—a century old and with good bones but stripped of its original features after a 1950s redo rendered it 'ranched' and in need of restoration, but I was spackled out.

Another move, this time to the corner of a repurposed flour mill famous for never having exploded. Just across the river from downtown Minneapolis, my cobblestoned street has an art-house cinema showing five-dollar films on Tuesdays and a major festival each April. I can see my publisher's building just across the river from here. My new local is dim, cozy, and hosts a free, curated singer-songwriter night each week. The coffee shop is named for Oscar Wilde. Best of all, the view is over the northern reaches of the same river Mark Twain set Huck Finn afloat on. Again living in history, this time on the National Register. The back bedroom features a section of a 'man-vator'—a vertical conveyance with foot and hand-holds that once moved mill-workers continuously up and down through the nine floors—just jump on and jump off (while praying, no doubt, it was all pre-OSHA). In the caverns below the street, watery catacombs now house a new turbine that spins electricity from skeins of water diverted from St. Anthony Falls. The building is a showpiece of repurpose, housing artists, musicians, *writers*. We endure flour beetles and photo shoots of wedding parties in our alley (nothing says forever like bridesmaids backed up against urban grit) and congressmen that don't believe artists deserve rent protections. We get to hear the clop of horse hooves on cobblestone while lying in bed, and live among artists. My neighbor's loft leaks soulful saxophone, the soprano practices in the atrium, and basement studios thump bass. From the window in my office I can watch the painters through the skylights in their shared studio. The rooftop has views to instill feelings of puniness for being the insignificant specks that we are, but also the comfort of thinking we might just have some integral role in something larger and grander than ourselves. Again, I live somewhere inspiring.

It's hard to compare one neighborhood or city to another when you love both. One thing Minneapolis and St. Paul share is a shortsightedness to their own attributes, like the handsome guy unaware that he is, which can be good—to a point. For a while, the Minneapolis city motto was "We Like It Here," which you can read as either drolly modest or protesteth too much-eth. By any national standard (save income and housing disparities, police shootings, and _____ (fill in your own blank)) we have it good in the Twin Cities. Writers have it extra good. One day high up on the rooftop taking in the far view, it struck me like a prospector spotting color. Literary gold, one bookish entity leading to another, a meandering path formed so steadily and slowly over the years that little notice has been taken— an amazing literary corridor lining both banks of the Mississippi River. A dozen publishers, the Minnesota Center for Book Arts, libraries, a literary center, the ivied halls of the University of Minnesota—all within several square miles. How many writers and wannabe writers have been tucked up in old lofts and garrets and dumpy student triplexes over the decades, tapping away in fingerless gloves (finally back in vogue a century after the Spanish flu) writing screenplays, tortured poetry, flash fiction, blogs, even books, hopefully. Monoliths of glass apartments keep popping up around us to shunt aside the very history and charm that led to the neighborhood's renaissance—but not so many as to obstruct the view to cultural riches, if you're looking.

Jon finally sold the old pickle baron's house and can now swap lawn work and to-do lists to play music and spend time in the studio and we can both get on with what really matters. A dozen years ago, I crossed over for love, and while it took nearly all that time to discover another writers' paradise, it's been here all along right under our noses. Like love often is. Finally, this Minneapolis deal is starting to feel like home.

Full Circle

MARGE BARRETT

In gratitude to the Loft Literary Center

I chose some classes to learn to write
my personal universal
tale in prose and poetry
years later became a
teacher with students
who chose to write
beside me
about
life

Seasons of Minneapolis

ADAM REGN ARVIDSON

Blue has no dimensions, it is beyond dimensions.
—*Yves Klein*

Winter

Snow falls in October. The public radio station devotes a whole hour to discussing the event, and listeners call in to ask when the earliest measurable snowfall occurred or what was the most snow the city ever got in October. Talk about the weather isn't just small talk here; it's a well-researched discussion, full of personal opinion, documented theses, and bold predictions. I don't think it strange anymore when the first snowfall of the year happens in October. I surprise myself by enjoying it, the way the snow hangs in the trees still spangled with the yellow and orange of autumn, the way it lays on pumpkin patches like a blanket on marbles, the way the people immediately commandeer it for their own fun: the making of six-foot snowmen, the strapping on of actual skis to replace the wheeled versions that die-hards have been training on for months, the dangerous racing on sleds down the park hills toward the not-yet-frozen creek. One winter, I meet a girl. A local girl. I trudge through the snow between her apartment and mine in the middle of the street, because the sidewalks are unreliable—some already cleared by ambitious homeowners with powerful snowblowers, others still buried in the drifts. During another oncoming winter, I marry the girl. In another, I snowshoe with her under the gnarled bur oaks in the park near the house we buy together. She pauses, smiles, her winter coat bulging at the middle with our first-born. I drive past the lake near our house on the way to pick up the new storm windows we ordered, and I am struck by the blackness of the water—a bottomless void in the white world.

Spring

This is called the City of Lakes. Minneapolis. The Lakota word for water; the Greek word for city. Private waterfront hardly exists here. Cedar Lake, Lake of the Isles, Nokomis, Harriet, Hiawatha, Bde Maka Ska, Minnehaha Creek, the Mississippi River: the big houses stare at these waters across public swaths of green through which meander slow parkways, bicycle trails, walking paths, and lush plantings of trees and shrubs, tirelessly maintained by the park board. I move here for a job. I am a young landscape architect and this city has a deep legacy. In the 1880s, H. W. S. Cleveland laid out these forty miles of waterside parkways. In 1916 came Theodore Wirth, the parks builder, who made wild bird sanctuaries, sledding hills, swimming beaches, and playgrounds. Theodore's son Conrad, who grew up in a house in a park near a lake, became director of the National Park Service in the 1950s and went on a building spree himself: visitor centers, trails, scenic overlooks. Conrad's son Ted, who visited his grandfather often in Minneapolis, built his own firm in Montana and designed park systems for the world: Riyadh, Kuwait, Nigeria. I am new here, and an anomaly. Most are from here and few leave. I walk the trails around Lake Harriet in forty-five degrees in shorts and a T-shirt.

Summer

The girl is a blue-eyed Norwegian redhead. A girl with a family who have lived here all their lives and who have a cabin up north. The natives all have cabins and have left the urban lakes for other lakes. The Land of 10,000 Lakes. 10,000 shards of summer sky reflected on the ground. Minnesota. Lakota for sky-tinted waters. The lakes become grass-tinted as the temperature rises, choked with algae feeding on the phosphorous we pour on our cabins' lawns. We mow to the shoreline and dump sand for our beaches on the reeds and arrowheads growing out in the water. The silence once broken only by loon calls we now break with the scream of Jet Skis. We campaign for a constitutional amendment to forever protect our right to hunt, fish, and trap. We sue the government to let us shoot wolves. When I married the girl, I married the family. I sit in traffic on Sunday afternoon on Highway 169 heading back to the city from Brainerd, our little boy, facing backward, unhappy, his lake-blue eyes squinched tight and soaking wet.

Autumn

The summer construction season is ending and I attend grand openings. The Walker Art Center is featuring Eiko and Koma: a Japanese couple lying naked in a gallery in a bed of feathers—for a month. I sit politely and watch them move at glacial pace, then file out without a word. I wander the halls of this giant steel cube, designed by Swiss architects Herzog and deMeuron to resemble folded paper cut through paper-snowflake style. I watch the videos of Yves Klein making his artworks: naked women bathing in International Klein Blue paint, then pressing themselves on canvases, leaving the blue outlines of hips, breasts. I stare into Klein's untitled blue squares and am pulled inward. Across town looms the Guthrie Theatre, another grand opening, designed by Klein's countryman Jean Nouvel. It sits above the river, a cobalt hulk at the scale of the hundred-year-old General Mills and Pillsbury grain silos that stored the flour that built this city. I walk out on the skybridge, a cantilever stretching out toward the Mississippi River. I think it an unnecessary extravagance but that it offers an incredible view. The river rushes hundreds of feet below me, hemmed in by locks and dams and the ruins of original sawmill and flourmill races. To my left the water slides down St. Anthony Falls, once the most quickly eroding waterfall in the world, now a concrete flume. To my right the river curves from view through the gorge, the only place in its entire length it is limited so tightly. Mississippi. Ojibwe for Great River. The leaves are changing. I am pretty far north, exactly halfway from the equator to the pole, and the summer light at 10:00 p.m. will soon give way to winter darkness at 4:30 p.m. I flee the city one last time to take the dock out of the water, pick Honeycrisp apples, navigate a corn maze.

Winter

The girl I married has eyelashes long enough to catch snowflakes. She stays fashionable in winter: sweater, scarf, long coat, tights, chunky Sorel snowboots. We move our car from one side of the street to the other and back, over three successive days, every time it snows, to let the plows clear the streets. Every storm is compared to the "Great Halloween Blizzard of 1991." Our two-and-a-half year-old son thinks a big *lizard* came to town last night. The city around us is dark but alive, grumbling about the slush, the chill, but reveling in the possibilities of skiing on the creeks, cuddling up near the heat of coffee shop hearths. My father-in-law takes me ice fishing. I always imagined it pointless and boring, but I find a certain Zen-like peace in it. The augur drills down into the lake to reveal a cylinder of blue, into which I drop my hooked minnow, weights, bobber, and I wait. After hours interspersed by sips of whisky, handfuls of canned mixed nuts, and bites of sandwich warmed in foil on the propane heater, my bobber plunges downward. My rod spins and I raise a crappie, speckled like a lake full of augur holes, cold and firm. I kill it with a blow to its head and hold it in bare hands like a chunk of ice, then toss it out of the shack to freeze. I learn that crappies taste better through the ice. I notice that the heavens and earth have reversed. The blue lakes of spring have iced and gone white. The hazy hot cloudy sky of summer has gone crystalline blue. I am reminded of Yves Klein, who wrote:

"*All colors bring forth specific associative ideas, tangible or psychological, while blue suggests, at most, the sea and sky, and they, after all, are in actual nature what is most abstract.*"

Even married into this place, ice-caught crappie in hand, I will never be from here. But I will find it difficult to leave, easy to love.

The Why

BAO PHI

At a prison reading
the majority of the audience was from my neighborhood:
the guys shouted out *Phillips*
as if welcoming home one they once thought alien.
A beautiful black transwoman asks for my autograph.
I want to ask her story, but she walks out smiling
with the loops of my name on a page
while I stand there silent.

They've come to listen to the art that kept me out of this place
but I'm still the one that gets to walk through those detectors
to whatever I call home.

Now I want my daughter
to have some record of this man—
sashimi-thin when the world doesn't want to see me,
fatty pork when they need to hate me—
they'll consume me and there will be only silence.

A book can be another empty space
I could have been, a ghost haunting the margin—
no words to describe himself.

Invisible Ink:
The Art of an Unfinished Life

JASON ALBERT

I. Outlining

We stood in the tiny entryway of Jackalope Tattoo, an all-female shop in Minneapolis. Tattoo machines buzzed behind us, smothering the acoustic drone from the speakers above. I had set an appointment with her months before, so I had plenty of time to hone my request. I had gone over it again and again in my head, perfecting my words. Still, my nerves pulsed. This wasn't a passing thought. I was going to ask her for a present for my son, one that would last forever. One day I could show him my tattoos, while telling him the story of how I almost lost him before I got the chance to know him.

Mo Richard waited. She wore black jeans and a black tank top, her arms blanketed with color. But there was no edge. Brown hair fell messy on her shoulders, her glasses slid down her nose. In every way, she projected a maternal warmth.

"It's for my boy," I said. "He was born far too soon and nearly died." Her soft brown eyes went big. "What I mean is, it's a happy thing. He's fine now. I want classic storybook art. Something old, washed out." I pointed at the disconnected black and gray line-art pieces on my forearm: the beaten and tired old man from *The Giving Tree*, a tiger wrestling a demon. I had gotten these tattoos from a different artist when my son's life was sustained by tubes and wires, when the worst was conceivable. "I want all of this tied together."

In some ways I felt we had already met. I had spent hours researching Mo and her work. I knew she had won awards, that she most often worked in an intersection of whimsy shot with darkness. Her animal skulls were anatomically stark, yet never grisly. She was just as likely to draw field mice in a tangle of raspberry bushes or an Audubon-inspired crane, as a pair of disembodied black-nailed hands reaching for a scarab. Her art teased charm out of the macabre, made it approachable.

I paused, frustrated. I was fumbling my practiced lines, knowing I wasn't telling her enough. But how could I ask of her what I really wanted? Can you please take these harrowing memories of mine, these fears, and make them less raw? Preserve both me and my son's vulnerabilities while also providing us safety?

"I wish I could describe exactly what I mean," I sighed. "But I don't know how. I just want happier stories."

She nodded and smiled, pushed her glasses up. "It's cool," she said. "Let's look."

I held out my arm while Mo studied. Then she reached for it, holding it gently, turning it palm up. She moved her finger through the air, drawing in her mind. "Don't worry," she said. "We'll come up with something good. We'll make a little world for all these guys to live in."

I found comfort in the "we," even though she was doing all the work.

Two weeks later I sat in her chair for almost five hours. She wiped away the blood from her needles. With each pass, the world she'd imagined came into focus. The old images stayed, but around them appeared robins and party banners and aquamarine flowers extending from the shadows. Grass and trees and bright blue clouds. She'd conjured an organic fantasia, filling the negative space with color, motion, and fairytales. Perfect in that it was nothing like what I'd described, yet when I thought of my son, now long since gone from the gloom of the neonatal ICU, I couldn't imagine it as anything other than what it had become. She had somehow softened the pain, while not making any attempt to hide it.

"This is so much fun," she said. "Thank you for letting me do this."

When she finished, the remembrance for my son now realized, I didn't think through my next move. I told her I wanted more. I didn't understand the urge consciously, only that there were other emotions and stories I needed to make permanent. And it could be no one but Mo to draw this memory map.

***

II. Shading

Over the next two years, Mo continued working up my arm, extending the storybook world she had conceived, creating new characters and fables. We would discuss ideas in broad concept, but I relied on her for the specifics—whatever made sense and felt right to her. The not-knowing was exciting, particularly when I was always sure that whatever she came up with would be right for me.

We sat together for close to thirty hours. We talked about her art, her longtime project drawing an entire Tarot deck, her many plants and pets. She talked about her husband, how they had a wild-hair dream of one day moving to South America. Just as often we spent long stretches in silence while she worked. Either way, it was always easy. Every time I left on a high, inspired to create something, anything. It was as much about being party to her artistry as it was the endorphins.

Custom tattoos are in many ways like therapy. There are no predrawn templates hanging on the wall to choose from, no perfect size or shape. The client has to open themselves up to their artist and explain not only what, but *why*. The artist has to be allowed to poke and prod. The client has to trust. They then channel the need and create a work that will fit on only one particular body. Imperfections and blemishes are considered and incorporated. If a piece is being inked too close to sensitive nerves, sessions are cut short. And because the best artists are in such high demand, it's common for there to be months between each sitting.

One session, we reached a spot on my shoulder she hadn't planned for. She had nothing ready.

"We have plenty of time left," she said. "What should we do?"

By now I expected the "we."

"Whatever you want," I said.

She reached for a sharpie and began sketching, her long, light strokes tickling in sharp contrast to the burn of her needle. Within minutes, she had finished. We stood in front of the mirror.

"It doesn't look like much of anything," she said, one more time moving her finger above the abstract twists and whorls she'd just drawn. It was as if she wanted me to see what she saw.

I shrugged. "Sure?"

"I know exactly what I'm going to do. It'll be good, promise."

She didn't have to promise. The idea of not trusting her was now so far distant, it seemed quaint that it had ever been a concern. This time she dreamed up a coiling flower colored in muzzled oranges and greens. An almost completely freehand work that was somehow both delicate and strong.

Whenever we finished a sitting, we had gotten in the habit of scheduling another as a matter of course. For the next one, moving over to my right biceps, I told her I wanted to memorialize my favorite grandfather. I talked about my still vivid memories of sitting in his lap as he taught me to play cribbage as a small boy, how he always made sure to act surprised when he let me win. He was a ceaseless smartass, a trickster spirit in the flesh.

"Something with a playing card would be fun," she said.

"I don't want a card. But maybe something *like* that."

She laughed. By now she knew better than to expect any more from me.

"We'll figure it out," she said.

***

III. Fade

We had a routine for our appointments. She would email her ideas to me the day before. Always late in the night, often after I had gone to sleep. It was a perfunctory act. Not only because it left no time for discussion or revision, but because there was never any need. She always seemed to understand what I was reaching for even better than I did.

By now the piece for my grandfather was half complete. She had inked a joker performing a one-armed handstand, throwing a fistful of confetti with his free hand. There were bluebirds again, and purple diamonds hanging in the sky like stars. Something *like* a playing card, but not.

But we still needed the second half. This was a story of a grandson, too. When we talked through it, I gave her even less than usual. It wasn't that I was out of ideas. At some point I had decided this would be my final tattoo, it was the last story I needed to carry with me in my skin. And I didn't want our friendship to end.

The night before our final sitting, she emailed me a drawing. It was too dark, too weird. I could have called and told her it wasn't for me. But I felt somehow responsible, so I kept my appointment, if only to deliver the message in person. And for the first time in years, I walked through the door and was struck by the same fat-tongued incoherence of my initial visit. I was afraid of letting her down, breaking our spell.

But I had barely begun to speak when she cut me off. She knew.

"It's okay, I get it. Sometimes it takes seeing what you don't want to know what you do. It's a beautiful day. I'll go home and work in my garden."

We set another date and I turned to leave. She said, "Hang on, you're going to give me something this time." Then she started asking questions, and coaxed out the essence I didn't know existed. We settled on an image that left us both excited. When we met again two weeks later, she outlined in black a boy, a cupid, standing in front of a ropey, twisted tree. He's reaching to the sky with a bouquet, the flowers framed against another diamond star.

"It's me," I said.

She smiled.

"This is a good place to stop," she said. "Let's finish the color next time."

"Of course." I still hadn't told her this was it. I was relieved to stretch it out, to have a next time.

A week before my appointment, I was lying in bed, half asleep, scrolling through the news. I came across a headline in Minneapolis's alt-weekly:

"Mo Richard, beloved Jackalope Tattoo artist, dies suddenly at age 31."

I read the article, my head filling with a dirty fog. I read it again and again, each time hoping for a different ending. It was incomprehensible. Not only was she gone, it wasn't even the type of accident that could safely be compartmentalized in the context of wrong place, wrong time. She died of an aortic aneurysm. Her heart had literally given out while she worked.

In the days after, an unexpected grief washed over me. It was true we had spent hours together, but we had never once spoken outside our roles as artist and client. And yet I still carried these creations—our creations spun from her mind and hands. Forever gifts that provided me comfort whenever I looked at them. And now, what could I ever give back?

I spent the following days scouring the Internet looking for memorials and celebrations of her life. As awful as it was to contemplate how this could happen to such a kind and decent person, I came to realize how she had understood what I had not. I read again and again how she loved all her clients and relished the opportunity to collaborate. That was what she left behind for everyone she touched. Mo understood that even tattoos aren't permanent. They only live as long as the life carrying them. But the act of creating something together can be indelible.

My only hope for Mo is that she has found a world as radiant as the one she gave me: with cherry-breasted birds flying high against bright blue clouds, and aquamarine flowers blooming from the darkness.

The First Winter

RAE MEADOWS

In the fall of 2010, we bought an old house in Minneapolis with leaded glass windows, hardwood floors, a fenced-in backyard, and a garage, walking distance to Lake Calhoun, across the street from Bryant Park. I loved that house, felt newly hopeful in it. After leaving our home in Brooklyn, my husband Alex and I had been on a self-granted writing sabbatical for several years in Madison. Now we had a child and it was time to get back to real life. Alex had a new teaching job. I had just finished writing a book. I was eight months pregnant and our daughter Indigo was about to turn three.

Indigo had asthma, an overwhelming number of anaphylactic food allergies, sensory processing issues, compromised vision in her left eye, and what we would come to learn was called Selective Mutism, an anxiety disorder that left her unable to speak except to me or my husband. She had never stayed with a babysitter or anyone else because she wasn't able to say if something was wrong. She could die from a bite of toast. I was in a constant state of high alert. The world was a minefield; danger lurked in the most mundane places. Other people's houses triggered her asthma, she broke out in hives from milk residue on shared toys, airplane seats needed a top-to-bottom wipe down. A lick from a dog had landed her in the hospital a year before. Indigo's anxiety, compounded by our own, came out in massive inconsolable meltdowns. To ease her transition to our new home we put up a green slide in the backyard. She picked out a big-kid bed and jungle animals for the walls of her new room. She got her own small rake to help me with the leaves.

When Olive was born, Indigo was with us in the birth center because she would not stay with my mom who'd come to help out. In the twelve hours from when we arrived to when we headed home with a new baby, winter had lowered its brutal hammer. It was only October. When we got in the car, my hips wedged between the two car seats in back, Indigo glanced over and asked, "Is it coming with us?"

That week we got a ticket for not properly shoveling the sidewalk in front of our house. By the time we went to clear the entrance to our garage, a three-foot wall of ice had formed from the plowed alley, blocking us from using it for the entire winter.

Alex went back to his classes and his colleagues. In my post-partum haze, single-digit temperatures outside, I was marooned in the house with a raging toddler and a fussy infant. While Olive slept I feverishly cleaned and dusted to keep Indigo's asthma from flaring. A trip to the grocery store was about as much as we could handle. I would return home, park on the snowy street, lug Olive in her car seat up the hill and the slippery front steps, set her down inside, and then take Indigo back outside with me to the car—she would not stay in the house—to retrieve the groceries. Inside we began the Sisyphean unbundling, peeling off snow pants and scarves and mittens that soon sizzled on the radiator. It was all I could do not to crawl into bed. More and more often, Indigo exploded in ferocious tantrums directed at me. When the daylight gave up, I would watch the clock, willing Alex to come home.

One gritty-eyed morning, up in the predawn darkness with Olive, the thermometer on our porch registering below zero, I watched a figure in a huge coat and boots lumbering around in the park across the street. He attached a hose to a spigot and soon steaming water arced out from the nozzle. He moved the hose left to right, left to right. It was hypnotic. For an hour, two. When the sun was up, I went to the window. A patch of smooth ice glittered where snow-covered grass had been. The man returned, morning after morning. It was a comfort to see him out there doing his patient, steady work. In a few weeks the park was transformed into a giant ice rink.

***

To have a reason to leave the house, I signed us up for a Music Together class, which was almost worse than doing nothing at all. Indigo would not dance and not sing and not throw scarves into the air. My false compensatory enthusiasm left me feeling unhinged. Olive would cry and Indigo's anger would erupt and we would scoot out to the car, through snowdrifts that spilled over the tops of my boots.

Therapist and doctor and allergist appointments filled the days. I searched out recipes for things that didn't include wheat, dairy, soy, eggs, nuts, peanuts, sesame, peas, mustard, lentils, fish, or shellfish. Pudding made from avocados and cocoa powder, cookies made from coconut flour, raisins, and xanthan gum. Around three o'clock the light grew orange and pale. Indigo and I sat and watched the skaters from our front window.

I had only skated once as a kid, but I decided to buy ice skates anyway.

One night after the girls were asleep I wrapped myself in my warmest gear and waved goodbye to Alex.

"Don't forget to come back," he said.

With my skate laces tied over my shoulder I walked across the empty street. The only light came from the streetlamps near the park. I sat in a snow bank, took off my mittens—my fingers quickly going numb—and laced up. I wobbled onto the ice and promptly fell on my knees. I shakily stood and slid my way forward. I didn't think of children or the writing I wasn't doing or meals or appointments or disappointments or loneliness or the blue darkness. I thought about bending my knees and keeping my ankles straight and not breaking my wrists. One full-frontal fall knocked the wind out of me, but, thankfully, no one was there to see it. I sat in the falling snow, found my breath, and got back up.

Night after night I went to the ice and skated around in the muted light. I taught myself to skate forward and backward. With long strides and smooth turns. Around me the city slept in all that quiet winter.

***

I swallowed my fear and enrolled Indigo in a two-day-a-week afternoon preschool. I sat outside in the car with Olive asleep in back, only once having to run in when Indigo had an asthma attack. She didn't talk to teachers or other kids, but neither did she fall apart. Her class played outside everyday unless it fell below ten degrees. I kept a view of the playground, trying to catch glimpses of what Indigo was like apart from me. I knew there were years of work ahead of us, but as another girl pulled her around in a sled, Indigo dragging her hand through the snow, I also knew that she didn't need me all the time. She was fragile, but she was strong, too.

Winter, that long and trying season, inched past. I met some preschool moms. I retired my uniform of Ugg boots and faded yoga pants. The ice in the rink grew cracked and pitted and the man with the hose stopped coming in the mornings to smooth it anew. My skates went up on a shelf in my closet. And in those first days of spring, when the light beat back the darkness and the tulips broke through what snow remained, I exhaled relief—we had made it. As the weeks went by, and the sun stayed longer and new green emerged all around us, I pushed the girls side-by-side in the playground swings and I felt better. I had started to feel at home.

Next winter I vowed to take Indigo out on the ice and teach her to skate.

***

The day came to move away again. I closed the front door of our house for the last time and cried all the way to the airport. We had only lived in Minneapolis for three years, but it felt like hard-won love. Olive and Indigo, now seven and ten, each wear a necklace with a Minnesota charm, a heart where Minneapolis should be. We come back to visit every year, but only in the summer, in that glorious amnesiac season when gliding across the frozen park, through the dark, seems impossible.

The Chain of Lakes

JAY BOTTEN

Cedar, Kenilworth
Isles, Calhoun, Harriet; flow
The path of glaciers

Life on an Urban Lake

JOHN ROSENGREN

Not long after we moved into our house on Lake Harriet, I noticed that every morning at 11:20, a white-haired man with a grizzled goatee parked his dented white pickup in front, hoisted two five-gallon buckets filled with bread crumbs out of the back, and crossed the street to feed the ducks. He showed up every day, snow or shine, even on holidays. That winter, our first on the lake, the ducks waited patiently for him. We never exchanged a word, but the stranger seemed as much a part of our lives as the ducks themselves. That's life on an urban lake.

I had always wanted a cabin up north. A place where I could hitch my hammock by the water, enjoy nature, and get away from it all. So when my wife was pregnant with our first child, we sold our condo on Bde Maka Ska and bought a house on Harriet. The family-oriented lake seemed the ideal place to sink roots and raise children. We moved into a crooked old stucco three-story built in 1915. Now, instead of packing up the car on Friday afternoons to head to the lake, we simply walk across the street any day of the week.

Each lake on Minneapolis's chain emits its own distinct personality. There's Cedar, with its nude beach and naturalist hikers. There's Isles, with its stately mansions and well-invested walkers. There's Bde Maka Ska, formerly known as Calhoun, anchored by its volleyball net and tattooed set. Then there's Harriet, ringed by residential neighborhoods, where moms jockey their strollers.

Rivers bring people places; lakes bring people to them. Like the daily duck feeder. Or the young guy in overalls—but otherwise bare-chested and barefoot—whom I saw walking every afternoon last summer. His blond beard reminded me of a flatland Jeremiah Johnson. Or the woman speedskater with the red helmet and blonde ponytail who sports a bikini top on hot days. Or the cigar-smoking baby boomer who hoists his bike off the rack of his green Lexus, then pedals and puffs on his way. Or the eccentric woman who rides a recumbent bike with her poodle snuggled against her chest in a baby carrier. Whether it be out on the paths, swinging in my hammock, or perched by the third floor window at my writing desk, I see a little bit of everything on this lake.

Situated as we are across the street from a city lake, our front yard becomes public property. Our lot sits on a corner, with a side street running along our property into the parkway, and its sidewalk carries a lot of foot traffic to and from the lake. We're not happy to see all of them. Watering dogs have killed a couple of small evergreens along the sidewalk. Ducks drop their business. One day this spring, I shooed an amorous trio (two drakes, one hen) of mallards across the street. But then they suddenly took flight back into the yard, swooping low at my head in their feathered revenge. I felt like I was trapped in a Hitchcock scene.

Sometimes, unexpected visitors show up. One snowy morning, I was writing upstairs at my desk when I heard a crash. I looked up to see a green Saturn crumpled against an ash tree in our front yard. By the time I got downstairs, a couple of passersby had pushed the car clear and tended to the driver, a young woman a bit shaken up, but otherwise unhurt, save for a small cut on her finger. I let her wash her hand at the kitchen sink and call her employer, then saw her off. Another winter morning, while clearing the night's snowfall from the sidewalk, I found an angel imprint left in our front yard, an anonymous gift.

The lake takes on a different character in winter. Snow forests the frozen surface and surrounding trails. The full moon rises heavy and yellow from the far shore and climbs high in the cold night sky. The moonlight bathes the snow in a soft glow and sparkles against our bedroom's frosted windowpanes. Tracks of all sorts mark the snow spread across the lake's surface: snowshoes, skis, sleds, dogs, even a truck out on an illegal joy ride. Crooked trails of footprints stretch from one shore to the other—no one seems able to walk the distance in a straight line.

On a warm winter afternoon, when the sun had melted open a small patch of water, my sister drove in from the suburbs with her kids, and we crossed the street to feed the ducks. We tossed bread crumbs onto the thin ice and watched the ducks skitter and slip across its glossy surface like Bambi on a greased log. A heavier goose fell through and slowly thrashed her way back to the open water. The woman who'd stopped to rest her puppy laughed with us at the sight.

For all I've gotten to know of this lake, it still holds its secrets. Take the white-haired man with the grizzled goatee who fed the ducks every day. I wondered why he did that, what his story was. I meant to strike up a conversation with him. But then one day, he stopped coming. I'm left to wonder what happened to him. Did he get sick? Pass away? He couldn't have just lost interest; habits like that die hard.

We'd love to stay in this house until our kids grow old, but we know that we won't live forever. We also know that long after we're gone, this lake will still wield its attraction and intrigue. So it should be with an urban lake.

On the Number 6 between Lakewood Cemetery and Lake Calhoun

JULIAN BERNICK

The softness is falling
And the winter is bright
Against the black trees
Of the morning light.

Alongside the lake
it settles on graves,
Where the buses roar by
The razor-gray waves.

I was young here
in this very place
And wore the dark morning
On my young face;

But old enough now
To know where we roam.
Beside the gray water
I can see my way home.

Crossing Over

MEGAN KAPLAN

The first border crossing I remember as a St. Paulite came one Sunday afternoon when my parents announced they were taking me and my younger siblings on a bike ride to Lake Harriet from our home in Crocus Hill. When I found out our destination, I could hardly get my Keds on fast enough.

Growing up in St. Paul in the eighties, Minneapolis was unknown territory. Twins residing on either side of the Mississippi, different as night and day, was the storyline in my six-year-old mind. The geographical setup of the cities had a mythic quality I held on to when our family first moved here from out of state. It was the kind of thing I could tell my buddies back home to explain the move: a welcome piece of trivia, a two-for-one.

But in the months after we arrived in St. Paul, I had yet to meet the sister city: the bigger, more boisterous one. From a scenic overlook along the east riverbank, Minneapolis's tree-lined side looked identical, but I knew it had its own alternate reality.

Crossing over was a "thing" I learned early on, and the jocular rivalry is still openly talked about. People from St. Paul usually come up with an excuse to get you to meet at their corner Irish bar; they roll their eyes over highway traffic. Folks living on the Minneapolis sideshow feigned interest: *I just never have a reason to go . . . What's the name of that one restaurant you like?*

When I was young, our family lived in New York, and we often took the train in from Long Island from the time I was a toddler. I was most comfortable in crowds, my arm stretched up as my mom pulled me up and over curbs. In the laid-back St. Paul neighborhood where we landed, life felt like a slow-building yawn in comparison—clean leafy blocks with the freedom to run and tumble, and not as much grit as I was used to.

That summer day we crossed the river to Minneapolis, my expectations were tucked into my bike basket as we rode miles along Minnehaha Parkway to Lake Harriet, coming upon a "palace" with turrets and flags, and teeming with people. There was the bandshell, perched on the water, and a big band shaking the roof down. We ate ice cream and popcorn for dinner. The sloping hill was packed with picnic blankets, a people-watching paradise. I felt at home.

As a teen, I kept crossing the river—on bikes, buses, borrowed cars. To know the two cities was to know opposite but attractive dating prospects. St. Paul was the dependable, affable guy with the tucked in shirt. Minneapolis had the sly untucked art of seduction. Down at the edge of the river in high school, we would drop kegs on the east side and hide out in the woods with plastic cups, watching our western counterparts light up the night with bonfires winking at ours.

On Sunday nights both sides converged at First Avenue in bodysuits, ripped jeans, and heavy eyeliner for the all-ages danceteria. There were the occasional murmurings of underagers getting into word-of-mouth Prince shows at Paisley Park, but Chanhassen was too far for most St. Paulites. Besides, First Avenue was the beacon of cool: meeting new friends from the other side behind the screens on stage, waving our arms to the Cure until they shut the music down.

I started saving up babysitting money so I could take the bus to Uptown. St. Paul's Grand Avenue had a sunny soup-and-sandwich vibe. But Hennepin oozed roasted beans and tap beer, and I longed to drink from that well. I also crushed on a guy who lived in an apartment off the 94 highway exit; his zip code being as attractive as anything else I can remember about him.

After college, I crossed over to live in a house on Bryant Avenue. We didn't realize it was a landmark until we saw cars parking out front, people getting out to pose for a picture where the Replacements had shot their *Let It Be* album cover on the roof. On the weekends, I'd haul my laundry over to St. Paul and slip into its quiet cocoon for the day, then head back over the river again to wait tables in the cacophony of downtown with career waiters, University of Minnesota grads, and drag queens who moonlighted at Gay 90's.

Later, after a bus boy I'd met (and would someday marry) and I spent several years working in New York, we decided to come home. The greener pathways, bursting restaurant scene, and unborrowed opportunities of the Twin Cities looked appealing.

"We'll look at both," we told our realtor when she asked us where we wanted to be. My parents were hopeful that we'd end up in St. Paul, closer to home. We drove around looking at lots, giving each city a fair chance, starving for the fresh air. But I knew deep down, just as I did as a kid, that Minneapolis was my place. It was the twin I identified with more, and maybe a commitment could be made. Within an hour, we were the owners of a small bungalow two blocks from the bandshell I'd set my eyes on that summer day years ago.

Eventually we all moved to Minneapolis, one by one, a family exodus: my sister, my brother, even my parents sold the Tudor we grew up in on Goodrich. The whole clan choosing one twin for another, a good conversation piece. *"I can't really find a breakfast place I like over here,"* my dad will say. *"It's nice that we have all these parks,"* my mom adds. The compare and contrast pinging back and forth. The best thing I've come to learn about twins—despite having favored one over the other—is that you've always got insurance, a backup sibling. That when you crave a change in the action, all you have to do is head to the river and cross it.

Hennepin and Lagoon, Minneapolis, 1984

JOSHUA DAVIES

Scotty grinds his deck along the ledge
Of the Walker Library
Artsy girls, skater boys scatter
From police into lonesome alleys
Beneath the railway bridge Gus's goons are drinking
Screaming out hardcore tunes
Knock-around, busting bottles on the tracks
In the swell and rage of youth
Boho saviors with a jaded faith
Percolate in the marquee café
Under theater lights their cycles fire the night
With the heat and hunger of dreams

Utopia burns in the mind, just behind
These hard and shimmering streets
We beat our hearts through
Realities torn apart
And embrace this city of life
We embrace in this city of life

Colleen's crashed with Smiley, Dillon, and Little George
In a squat just down the tracks
Pizza place dumpsters, melons stolen
From the market feed this runaway life
Suburban kids moth the flame of the trends
In the papers and on MTV
An innocence they feel never ends—
Photos of lives lost, faded glories

But the pictures don't feel the desperation
Or claw their way through the isolation
Don't communicate the revelation
We find in each other
And behind every song

Punks they dance on car roofs Uptown
To the soundtrack from *Purple Rain*
While yuppies line up at William's Nightclub
For a dose of immortality
Gawkers flock shop windows and bars
Flood the avenue's arteries
Everyone's alone; no one's ever home
Searching for somewhere, someone else to be

All I need to do is look to you
To know all I dream inside is still true
The discontent, the illusions undo
Every time I look at you
(I'm still / looking / for you)
Utopia burns in the mind, just behind
These hard and shimmering streets
We beat our hearts through
Realities torn apart
And embrace this city of life
We embrace in this city of life

Wall of Sound

LARS OSTROM

The refrigerator in our south Minneapolis home has concerns. It lets us know with a persistent, high-pitched beep. The door is open, the filter is shot.

From across the room, my wife Sara shoots me an exasperated look. "Can't you hear that?"

I'm sitting closer to it than she is, but the answer is no. A decade in the Minneapolis rock scene left me with tinnitus. Both ears ring constantly, a high B natural.

"I think you're going deaf," my son, Mason, says, as he gets up to deal with the beep. He is fourteen-years-old and unafraid to state the obvious. His younger sister, Sadie, comes to my defense. "He can't help it, he was in a band."

I hope I'm not going deaf. I hope the ringing is the only price I'll have to pay for thousands of hours standing in front of full-blast amps, pressed up against a drum kit, squeezed into a tiny practice space that smelled like an ashtray with a drinking problem.

But let's be honest. The damage is done.

***

My first band came together awkwardly. All four of us were overachieving college kids with hazy ideas about music and very little experience. Then we booked our first show at the last minute and had to learn forty songs in two weeks. I was assigned to the bass, even though I had never played bass before. (We already had two guitar players and I was the youngest.) The strings were the same, I thought, and it would be easier than soloing, anyway.

We had no idea what we were doing.

That show was on Valentine's Day, 1993, at a dive bar in Dundas, Minnesota. I had to lie about my age to Don, the booker, who owned the bar and lived upstairs. It was my first public performance of any kind since a piano recital in second grade, after which I had fainted. Anxiety flooded my stomach. I had pages and pages of cheat sheets. I was playing a borrowed bass through a borrowed amp. My hands shook.

Miraculously, everything worked out. Friends showed up, drank beer, and cheered us on. Our originals sounded better than they ever had at practice, and we ripped through cover after cover, including a countryfied version of "Back in Black."

Everyone was happy except Don.

Halfway through our set, he pulled us aside to say we were just too loud. We had to turn down because his elderly mother was recuperating from surgery upstairs and we were driving her crazy. He pointed upwards, indicating that this poor woman was trying to sleep directly above us.

Don had no idea what he was doing, either.

***

After college, the drummer moved back to Iowa and the rest of us moved to Minneapolis. One guitar player got into medical school and the other one, Eric, recruited his brother to play bass. I switched to guitar and we tried to find a decent drummer, which is harder than it sounds.

The first guy seemed normal enough. He could play. He showed up on time. We practiced in a cramped little room a block off University in St. Paul. Our sound wandered in the same neighborhood as Soul Asylum and the Replacements. Loud, snot-nosed guitar rock with heartfelt lyrics and a dash of don't-give-a-shit. We called ourselves Third Wheel, outsiders in what felt like an overly insular scene.

We booked our first show at a house party near the University of Minnesota and the drummer promptly quit. A friend of a friend volunteered to sit in, but there wasn't enough time to learn everything. We went on first in the middle of a crowded party. I expected to clear the room, but for three songs we hung together and rocked it out. Strangers applauded and inched closer.

Then I broke a string, and nothing sounded right after that. Both guitars went out of tune, Eric couldn't hear himself through the PA, and the drummer forgot how the songs ended.

Despite the rocky performance that night, I worked up enough courage to start talking to a woman I didn't know. I caught her eye in passing while we were packing up our gear, then tapped her on the shoulder just as she was about to leave. She had a side-shaved bob and wore wild blue floral leggings. She was just starting a band called Mollycuddle.

She was a singer and her name was Sara.

***

Just as Third Wheel hit its stride, Eric needed to go back home to work construction with his dad for a few weeks. At the same time, Jeff, an acquaintance, was looking for a bass player. Now that I had finished a few shows without passing out or throwing up, my confidence was stirring, so I signed up.

In Third Wheel, Eric wrote the songs, deftly capturing small-town life and big-time frustration. In this new power trio, we improvised songs in the moment. Everything was chaotic and fast. We called ourselves Supermodel because that word had just entered the cultural consciousness and it sounded appropriately ridiculous. We went through two drummers before we found Beef, a journeyman with fast hands and high stamina. He had toured extensively with his last band, painted houses for a (sort of) living and wore a "Cheese-a-saurus Rex" T-shirt. He had given himself his own nickname. He was perfect.

Supermodel was relentless and abrasive, like Jimi Hendrix fronting the Melvins. We were once handed a note during a show. Scrawled on a bar napkin, it read, "YOU GUYS ARE WAY TOO LOUD."

I'm quiet by nature, a shy and risk-averse person with a crippling fear of public speaking. But playing in a loud band shook something loose. It gave me permission to flail around and freak out and not worry about anything aside from what I was playing. Nerves hit me hard before every show, but they always disappeared behind the wall of sound. I played aggressively, my knuckles catching the strings, the bass spattered with my own blood.

***

Band life is a time suck. Practice and more practice. Booking shows. Hanging flyers. Playing shows. Listening to music. Writing songs. Drinking and hanging out and losing track of time. Going to bed at 2:00 a.m. and getting to work five hours later. It was pre-Internet, pre-cell phone. Everything took longer and was a giant pain in the ass. It was fantastic.

When you're in two bands at the same time, the cost is heavy. I was practicing four nights a week and playing four shows a month. When your girlfriend is in a band too, date night has to be cleared with three separate band calendars. Somebody is always mad.

Third Wheel finally found a great drummer, Chris, who solidified our sound. Eric's brother quit and we added Brian, a childhood friend of mine who had recently moved to town. The four of us clicked. Together, we went from playing for a handful of people on a Tuesday at Blues Alley (RIP) to a couple hundred people on a Friday night at the Turf Club.

Supermodel followed a similar trajectory, earning a reputation for oddball cover choices (like a sludged-out, half-time version of ZZ Top's "Got Me Under Pressure") and sheer volume.

Our aspirations were simple: go on tour and play bigger clubs, which we did. As far as we were concerned, we had done what we set out to do. Making a career out of it was never part of the plan.

***

Third Wheel and Supermodel ended on back-to-back nights in December of 1999. Eric had a baby at home. Jeff burned out. At a certain point, loading your gear back into the practice space at 2:30 a.m. on a Thursday loses its appeal.

I took a few months off. Sara and I went out to dinner, watched movies, walked around Lake of the Isles. We were newly married and thinking about buying a house. I read a book every now and again. I actually slept for more than five hours at a time.

And then we went to see Har Mar Superstar at the Weisman Art Museum. Outside, I started talking with Jason, the drummer from Har Mar's recently defunct noise rock band, Calvin Krime. He asked if I still played guitar.

Yes, I said.

Did I want to get together and play sometime?

I don't know, I thought. I looked at Sara. She looked back with a raised eyebrow.

Yes? I thought.

Yes, I said.

***

Exercise was noisy, angular and weird, a post-punk riot. It was also the loudest band I ever played in. To keep up with the bass player, I ran my guitar through a 300-watt bass cabinet. This was, by anyone's estimation, unbelievably stupid. It was also the best my Les Paul ever sounded. And if I turned the volume knob past two, the whole thing became a sonic weapon.

But now it was my turn to be the old guy in the band. The young dudes liked to drink, so much so that we could not book ourselves as a headliner because we would be too wasted to perform. Occasionally, these guidelines were ignored.

The guys also knew people in the local scene. Instead of hustling for every gig, we got invited to play. We opened for punk legends Dillinger Four at the Seventh Street Entry, but the crowd didn't quite know what to make of us. Our singer, Preston, wore novelty underwear with a talking monkey head on the crotch. At one point, Arthur the bass player jumped up and ate a spider that was descending toward the stage.

Our burn rate was high. We played a "best new bands" showcase at First Avenue. We put out two records with a local label. We toured.

Then our singer announced he was moving to LA.

We were done.

He'd stolen my thunder: I was about to tell everyone Sara was pregnant.

***

Not long ago, Eric from Third Wheel sent me a text on Record Store Day. It read: "Look what my daughter just picked up." Attached was a picture of his teenager, Ava, holding a Supermodel seven-inch single. I recognized one of the song titles; the other two were a mystery. What really came back was the recording session, two days spent at a freezing studio located inside a converted grain silo in 1997.

For the next hour, I fell into a nostalgic vortex, listening to old music with fresh ears. Songs I recalled as fast and powerful sounded rushed and clumsy. Slow ones I remembered as plodding now seemed thoughtful and patient. But the hits were still the hits. I knew exactly where I would have put them on the set list.

***

"Seriously, Dad. Can't you hear that?"

It's my daughter Sadie bugging me again about the beeping refrigerator. She is doing her homework and would prefer not to be disturbed. At age eleven, she already has a wonderful singing voice, strong songwriting instincts, and enough personality to be a lead singer like her mom.

I've already decided that if she joins a band, I will try to hold back on the unsolicited advice. I will try and restrain myself from reliving my glory days, name-dropping bands, bending her ear about guitars and amps and, most importantly, earplugs.

I will try and I will surely fail.

I can't hear the refrigerator. I never can, and never will. But I get up quickly and take care of it, so she doesn't have to.

"Yes, I can hear it now," I tell her. "I can hear it all."

Purple Rain

LUISA MURADYAN

In the Talmud there is an angel
whispering to every blade of grass: *grow, grow*
In the other world, Prince whispers to every dove: *cry, cry*
and when he asked me about the status of my searching
I nodded and told him I had been purified
in the waters of Lake Minnetonka.
Here's the thing about wearing a blouse—
you put it on one sleeve at a time,
become a man one silver hoop earring
at a time. I've never understood why
God gave us five fingers on each hand
when I would have made do with two.
Those were the fingers with which you
touched my outstretched hand
when I was made into a woman
the ceiling of the Sistine chapel
painted with your raspberry tongue.

Homeboy

J. D. FRATZKE

When the kitchen at the hotel restaurant in Minneapolis had been cleaned, the stoves and lights off, the demi-glace simmering in the steam kettle overnight, we would feel gutted and grimy, but hyper-tuned. We'd head down the street to a bar, and two cocktails into debriefing the night, we'd end up debriefing our lives.

"At the last place I worked . . ."

An endless round-robin of war stories. Many of us, three or four kitchens into our career, would laugh at one another, knowing we had no choice in the matter anymore. We were hooked. Seared. Lifers. Sous chef someday, maybe in a year or two, chef in another five if we could hack it, when we would be ending our nights just as beaten up but in a different, deeper way—asking ourselves the same question we were asking each other now: "How did we get here?"

One of the most influential chefs in American history, Norman Van Aken, is often credited with the adage, "This is not a business you choose, it chooses you."

I didn't choose this business. So when I ask myself, "How did I get here?" I always come up with the same answer.

It was Chef Rick.

A friend of my girlfriend had left her job at a sandwich shop and I needed to get out of minimum wages at the record shop where I was working. My modicum of experience at the Dinkytown Market Deli probably qualified me for the seven bucks an hour the owners were paying, so I jumped at it. Having just dropped out of college, the debt I was incurring was now up to my thighs. Loyalty? Yeah. Yessir. I had nothing planned for that day, or the next, or ever beyond the perfect turkey on rye.

The establishment on Hennepin looked closed at 4:00 p.m. but I tried the door, found it open, and crept in. No one was there. The tile was bright and all the tables were set, but the lights were down. My eyes shifted to the right and took in the length of the deli case. In shadows it looked half a block long. I imagined the lunch rush, packed to the gills, a scenario like the entire floor of the Wall Street stock exchange screaming at me over the counter for three hours a day. (*I SAID POTATO SALAD NOT POTATO*

CHIPS YOU SMALL TOWN HICK MORON!) At nineteen years of age, the only high volume I wanted was in my car stereo. I turned around to walk out as the kitchen doors near the entrance flew open.

A stocky silhouette immediately blurted, "Hey, can I help you?"

He was wearing what I knew was a chef's coat and baggy checkered pants. I quickly averted my eyes to his shoes (because I had been raised Lutheran and in Minnesota, that's the law). They looked like a Dutch clown had tried to fashion clogs out of old truck tires with a dull hammer. I have since come to know them as Birkenstocks.

He introduced himself as Rick, shook my hand, and handed me an application for the restaurant in the Rogue Nightclub downstairs, explaining that they shared a kitchen with the deli. I told him I'd never worked in a real restaurant kitchen.

"Look," he said, "Just go ahead and fill it out. I need some daytime help. You've done food before and I prefer to hire prep cooks with no experience. That way I don't have to break any bad habits."

The next morning, my phone rang and Chef Rick asked when I could start.

Three days later, I was wearing a coat like Rick's and pants like Rick's while he toured me through the coolers . . . This is where we keep the herbs. Do you know herbs? No? Okay, this one's thyme. Rub it between your fingers. Nothing else in the world smells like that. Now basil. Oh, you know basil? Cool. You like it? Yeah, me too. My favorite on pizza. Rosemary? Here. Looks like a Christmas tree, right? Tarragon . . . Each one shoved under my nose, on and on for half an hour. I'd never heard of hummus. I tasted hummus. Rick taught me all about hummus. Rick made me make hummus. We served it with shrimp. I learned to thicken cream for a pasta sauce by boiling it, first high, then low, waiting to add the fresh ingredients at the end. The kitchen didn't have a mixer so all the whipped cream for desserts had to be whipped by the new guy, me, by hand, like my grandma did at Thanksgiving. Only grandma didn't teach me that it's a lot easier when the bowl and whisk are frozen and the cream is cold . . . Rick did.

After that day, my first day, the only place I wanted to be was there. I would show up early and read in the break room for hours, completely safe. Waiters asked me what I was reading and told me they preferred *Steppenwolf* to *Demian*. Everyone seemed to love music. Half the staff was either in a band or in between bands or in law school or worked in oils on canvas. Several of them had recently been released from treatment and were trying to start their rough lives over.

Nobody minced words. All the talk was direct. One day while we were suiting up for the shift, Chef Rick admonished the lead line cook for making fun of my chrysanthemum tattoo, explaining that Japanese royalty considered it a symbol of strength. These were my people. I had found a home.

Chef Rick eventually moved on, but I did not. I stayed for another two years before the club closed, moving back and forth between cooking and barbacking, working a half dozen other kitchen jobs on the side. I kept looking for better wages, more talented teachers, smaller and smaller kitchens. I kept building on what I had been taught, sometimes biting off more than I could chew. Failing. Losing jobs. Losing friends. Losing girl-friends. Starting fresh. Setting goals and fighting for them. Finding myself, over two decades later, with a far larger life than that nineteen-year-old ever thought he'd have.

I haven't spent many days in kitchens without thinking about Chef Rick. I've tried very hard to offer everyone in my kitchens the time, respect, and dignity he offered me. I have gone out of my way, often to a fault, to hire inexperience as a way to pay forward the life this business gave to me. I also find that teaching basics gives me the fresh eyes to reassess whether or not something we're doing can be done better.

I haven't seen Chef Rick for some time, but I know he's still running a kitchen somewhere. He represents, to me, the best of what this business can be; an opportunity to exercise knowledge and kindness, to be creative, nourish our world, and care for both the people who enjoy our food and the ones that help us prepare it.

Maya Angelou told us that "People will forget what you said and forget what you did, but they will always remember how you made them feel." Chef Rick made me feel like I belonged, and like the kitchen was my home. That is all I'll ever want my kitchens to be.

Lake Street Teppanyaki Grill and Supreme Buffet

MARCIE RENDON

Seasoned by parents' voices
Spanish, English, Somali, Arabic, Hmong
Children's words waft across steaming trays of international flavored air
Sushi, pho, dumplings, rice,
Raw shrimp, fried shrimp, breaded shrimp, shrimp cocktail
Steak, chicken, and hamburger sliders

Hijabs sit back to back
With long-skirted Guatemalan grandmothers fixing the strap
on tiny granddaughter's black patent leather kitten heels;
As fine leather-coated Arab men, stylish but not Minnesota warm,
Flirt with slender, long-sleeved, covered beauties

The world is dining here
Jell-O, mandarin oranges, pineapple,
Mangos, kiwi,
Pastries not sold at the local market
Fried rice, white rice, sticky rice, wild rice
Mashed potatoes, French fries, Minnesota scalloped potatoes

I don't see anyone eating with chopsticks
Lots of fingers licked, paper napkins crumpled
Plate after plate filled, eaten
Everything America has to offer

Having been to branded coffee shops for meetings
To corporate chains for steak and lobster
The Global Market for Swedish rye sandwiches
All these places,
but it was at the Teppanyaki Grill
That I found my people

The ones who scrimp and
Put on their best Savers finds for a night out
Who gather up the children, those in infant seats and sullen teens
Because family night out is family night out, dammit
And even if it takes a whole paycheck
Tonight, the family will eat supreme

Eating Halva on Lake Street

JAMES NORTON

It's February and I'm walking down East Lake Street in Minneapolis, approaching Bloomington Avenue. Ahead of me is the illustrator known as WACSO, who wears the lovingly distressed style of a mid-career rock musician. His business partner and friend, MC Cronin, walks at his side. Next to me is my wife, several months pregnant with our second child.

It's dark out, and the street is mostly empty. Tonight we will eat at five restaurants. This is about the thirtieth time we've done this, and we're closing in on two hundred spots that we've visited, drawn, tasted, and written about. We've done Central Avenue, and we've done University Avenue—East Lake Street is just our latest patch of turf. Some nights we eat at more than five places. We are tired, but still hungry.

***

Before moving to Minnesota, I spent about seven years living in Boston and New York. Not long after moving here, I attended a memorial performance in honor of the comedian Mitch Hedberg. After the melting pots of East Cambridge and Brooklyn, I was stunned by all the white faces. The room was young, well-groomed, and monochromatic, something I see over and over again here: at restaurants, at museums, at concerts, and while walking through the sometimes disconcertingly empty downtowns.

White as they were, the crowd meant well. One B-list comedian bombed hard by telling a series of jokes that were nothing more than stilted appeals to racial stereotypes. Blacks, Asians, Jews—everybody vulnerable got a turn. The crowd was stone-faced, the comedian increasingly panicked. "Good," I thought. "Screw this guy." He moved on, going after American Indians: "When I was in high school, my teacher asked us to sit Indian-style, so I drank a bottle of vodka and passed out in the gutter."

Huge laugh. Rollicking response. The comedian had won back the crowd. I looked around the room, my eyes bugging out in shock. Where was I? What was going on?

***

The point of eating at every restaurant in a place like Lake Street is that you'll walk into situations you would never knowingly choose. You'll go into restaurants without menus, where mayonnaise sits out at room temperature, where everybody in the place but you is from the same province thousands of miles away in Southeast Asia, or Central America, or East Africa.

Somehow it never fazes WACSO. He chats with everyone. Race, religion, age, gender—there are no dividers. He wears the uniform of American pop music but chats with people cheerfully, openly, even gently, and they open up. Tonight we're at an East African place that has only been here for a few months. We've never heard of it, and it seems to be a strictly first-generation-serving-first-generation kind of joint. It's our favorite kind of restaurant— the hospitality will be warm and the food good enough to serve to family.

WACSO has done some advance work, schmoozing with the guys in the front room—what are you eating? How long has this place been here? Are you guys here every week? The proprietors are ready to seat us up front amid all the action until they spot Becca, and then we're whisked off to the glorified broom closet of a "VIP room"—a place for Westerners who insist on dining with mixed genders.

***

I grew up in Wisconsin, eating lasagna and bratwurst and beef stroganoff and pizza. A light came on when I took a bus to Chicago with my high school Japanese class and ate my first piece of sushi. Seaweed, raw fish, vinegared rice—these were three things I'd never tasted before, and now I was tasting them all together at once. It kicked open the door to a lifetime of traveling on my stomach. Walking down Lake Street is just another leg of the journey.

There's an idea floating around about what "American" means. "American as apple pie" gets at it—there's a right way to eat, there are foods that are "normal," there are ways to fit in. It's prescriptive garbage, and it's hateful, and whenever I write about food I try to get to the point that good food is whatever feeds the soul, and that authentic food isn't about a canonical recipe. It's about the reason that motivated the cook to make the meal. People feel comfortable when things fit into categories, but the categories are illusions, and the illusions can hurt people and obscure the truth.

Personally, I am Jewish, but not very convincingly—enough to be a citizen of Israel or get sent to the death camps, but not enough to know much past Judaism 101. I've been the whitest guy in the room more times than I can count, and I've been given the hairy eyeball at brunch in Wayzata, at Scandinavian folk dinners, at press events, where something about me—a predilection toward talking with my hands?—triggers an internal alarm. So I think about categories a lot, and have for much of my life.

These days half of America is obsessed with tearing down privilege, and half of America wants to put up walls and rip apart families. I think about this stuff constantly as I eat, and as I write, and as I look at maps of where we've been and where we're going to go.

I don't want to be a tourist, I want to be a traveler. I want to tell people that a *cabeza* taco or a dollop of hummus is as American as apple pie, and maybe more so if you believe that we are a country of immigrants and refugees banding together to shelter under some clear-headed and big-hearted ideas.

***

The key dish at this Somali restaurant is something called halwo.

"Sounds like halva," I say, tapping into my bucket-sized reservoir of Jewish food lore.

What comes out is a hazard cone-orange, rubbery sweet that is evocative of clove and cardamom. It's served like a particularly deluxe jelly next to dry butter cookies, which are a natural complement. In the front of the house, among the men, the halwo is eaten with Ritz crackers.

Later in the evening, when I get back home and I'm trying to turn my notes into food criticism, I google around and find out that, sure enough, halwo is just another transliteration of halva, and halva is a category of sweets big enough to contain multitudes. I know this from two trips to Israel, but it's in East Africa, too, and the Caucasus, and Malta, and beyond in myriad flavors and textures. And now it's here in Minneapolis.

Even if you don't travel the world, the world finds its way to you on your plate. The more gracefully we taste the food that's new to us, the more warmly we talk to the people who make it, and the more willingly we cross the thresholds of restaurants that dot our avenues, the more completely we'll know where we're living. This is straightforward in theory but difficult in practice, with the goal being much more than the taste of food—it's the taste of fellowship.

And that is damn delicious.

Beauty Supply

DOBBY GIBSON

On the 21 bus this morning,
I noticed the Natural Braid & Beauty Supply
store on Lake Street
had a handmade sign in its front window
advertising *Front Lace Wigs and Fittings by Relyndis.*

I love Relyndis for daring to believe
that beauty can be supplied,
for believing in everything the used car dealers
farther down Lake have given up on,
beginning with the silver balloons and streamers
that disappeared once the economy went south.

Above the beauty supply store
there's a billboard for the Washburn-McReavy Funeral Home
advertising *Quality and Value Cremation Services,*
three white and white-haired men
in matching gold ties as shiny as the handles
of the three caskets I've lifted in my life.

There's Hymie's Records, where I found the Buck Owens LP
I'm unashamed to admit
I love listening to
at least partly because it smells of an oddly comforting
mildew from a stranger's basement.

I was born on this street, about a mile from here,
and can still take it almost all the way to the house
where my parents live,
just beyond Minnehaha Creek,
my beautiful dad in his beautiful basement
listening to the TV at a volume that would scare a soldier.

On Lake Street, there's the station
where I catch the downtown train
to use these words I love so much
for purposes I occasionally don't.

I never thought I'd live here.
The other day, when I drove Tony down Lake Street
and pointed to the hospital where I was born,
he said, "Your life is one of shocking continuity,"
and I wondered whether I was being given
a compliment or a warning.

I wonder if it was twenty-four degrees
on the day I was born, as it is today,
and if the light sank like it is now,
the traffic vanishing after dinner.

I wonder if, in another forty years,
my wife and I, and my daughter, and Relyndis,
and a half million other people like us
will still flush our toilets
into the river one last time before bed

as a new set of old used cars sleeps unsold on Lake Street,
and whether there will be another version
of the man with a limp
to shuffle out after the snow falls
to gently brush them off.

Party Bus

PEGGY "PEARL" ZAMBORY

This is not my first party bus. I don't know if this is a personal problem, or because I live in Northeast, but I have been on several. This one, rented for Jodi's fortieth birthday, is pink and black, inside and out. The seats all face the center, where a stripper pole has been installed. Our pony-tailed driver used to be bouncer at the Cabooze, and still wears his leather biker jacket.

It is early spring, with a chill in the air, and twenty-some women are aboard. We are friends, and we are all in various stages of drunken camaraderie as we go from pub to pub while the sky turns dark.

The evening has taken on a warm, smoky glow.

"My name is Louis," the driver had said. "This is a party bus, a drinking, dancing, smoking bus. Dance, laugh, shout. You need cigs? I'll stop. You need something at a convenience store? I'll stop. Keep all your bits inside the bus, and let's not attract more attention than a black and pink bus already does. Now let's have a good time!"

This is not, of course, the trusty number 17, my workaday Metro Transit Bus from Northeast Minneapolis to downtown Minneapolis.

This is not a commute.

This is an adventure.

Full of the love of a well-run pub crawl, the sun has gone down, the music has been turned up.

"I THOUGHT I SPOTTED A HIPPIE," LouAnn shouts at me. We have similar dance moves—reruns of *Soul Train* come to mind—and we high-five.

"I GOT ABOUT SEVEN INCHES CUT OFF ABOUT A MONTH AGO," Megan yells, flipping her hair from one side to another. "YOU DON'T THINK IT LOOKS CHOPPY?"

"I'M GONNA SECOND-HAND SMOKE MYSELF TO DEATH OVER HERE, MAN," shouts Kim. "BLOW IT OUT A WINDOW, ALREADY! NO. I TELL YOU WHAT—KEEP IT UP. I'M GONNA GO IN THE NEXT BAR, EAT A LOAF OF BREAD, AND ME AND MY GLUTEN ALLERGY ARE GONNA CLEAR THIS WHOLE BUS. YOU FEEL ME? YOU'RE JUST ONE SLICE OF BREAD AWAY FROM THE GASSY EXPERIENCE OF A LIFETIME."

The pink and black bus slides slowly, majestically, down the cobble-stoned roads to the river, down by the Grain Belt sign.

Diana hands me a beer. "HISTORIC MINNEAPOLIS."

I nod, move across the aisle from one side of the bus to the other to sit next to her. I lean in dramatically. "Can I just tell you that I've been drinking?"

"You could tell me," she says, "but I wouldn't beli—*hic!*—I wouldn't beli—*hic!*—I would be disinclined to have faith in your assumption."

We grin at each other. "Nicely done," I say.

She shrugs. "English is my native language."

We twist in our seats, look out the windows of the bus to the brick, to the river, to the stark beauty of the leafless trees against the starlit skies.

Behind us, music I don't recognize throbs, bass-heavy. Beautiful women dance in the aisle, shouting encouragement and jokes. Outside, Minneapolis moves silently from winter to spring.

Diana wraps her arms around me, and I rest my head on her shoulder.

"We are the luckiest women in the world," she says.

I nod. "I am inclined," I say, "to have faith in your assumption."

On 2ⁿᵈ Street Northeast

FRANCINE MARIE TOLF

It's that brief season when trees
are still bare-limbed but whispering green
for the buds clinging to nude branches.

I walk through my neighborhood,
a woman of nearly sixty
with no fresh wisdom to share,

but I must tell you that from a distance
this young tree might appear
a cloud of light green

while up close, each bud is so crisp and distinct
I could count the number of them
on every branch.

The Forgotten River

JONATHAN RABAN

I had crossed and recrossed the Mississippi. There were eighteen bridges over it in as many miles, and it seemed that already I had been on most of them. Yet I was having almost as much trouble as de Soto or La Salle in actually reaching the riverbank. Once, the Mississippi had provided Minneapolis and St. Paul with the reason for their existence. Later, it had turned into an impediment to their joint commercial life, to be spanned at every possible point. Now it wasn't even an impediment. The Twin Cities went about their business as if the river didn't exist. No road that I could see led down to it. From a gloomy little bar on First Street, I could smell the Mississippi, but didn't know how to reach it. Feeling foolish, I called the bartender over.

"How exactly do I get down to the Mississippi?"

"The river? She's on the far side of the tracks." The *wrong* side of the tracks. The river had been consigned to the part of town classically set aside for the American poor. It belonged to the same category as vandalized public housing projects, junked automobiles, and dead cats. I was appalled. No one would have dared do such a thing to the river in my head.

I left my beer untouched. Across the street, there was a potter's field of ancient railroads. Most had died. Others were in that geriatric state where death is just a whisker away. It was a sorry strip, half a mile wide, of dingy grass, cracked ties and crumbling rails. The rolling stock looked as if it had rusted solid on its tracks. I couldn't see any locomotives, only the names of the surviving railroad companies, painted in flaky lettering on the sides of the cars: BURLINGTON NORTHERN. CHICAGO AND NORTH WESTERN. MINNESOTA TRANSFER. THE SOO LINE. CHICAGO, MILWAUKEE, ST. PAUL, AND PACIFIC. Crickets wheezed and scraped at my feet as I crossed from track to track. The soggy holiday air smelled of diesel oil, rotting wood, and river.

I clambered between two standing chains of freight cars, slid down a culvert of cinders, and there was the Mississippi. All that I could see at first was what it was not. It was not a great glassy sweep of water, big enough to make the civilization on its banks look small. It wasn't the amazing blue of the cover of my old copy of *Huckleberry Finn*. Nor was it the terrible chocolate flood of Charles Dickens and Frances Trollope.

It was just a river. From where I stood, the far bank was no more than a couple of hundred yards away. Its color was much the same as that of my domestic Thames: a pale dun, like iced tea with a lot of mosquito larvae wriggling in the glass. I squatted moodily on a bleached rock, looking across at the dead smokestack of a Victorian mill, and listening to the rumble of a weir upstream. I lit a cigarette to frighten off the gnats buzzing in a thick cloud around my head and flipped the empty pack into the river. The surface of the water was scrolled with slowly moving eddies. My cigarette pack drifted for a moment, slipped into the crease of an eddy, and was taken crabwise off the stream. How long, I wondered, would it take to reach the Gulf of Mexico? Two thousand miles at . . . what—four, five miles an hour? A month? Six weeks? At any rate, it would arrive long before I did. I watched its red flip-top lid slowly circling in the tepid water until it was carried out of sight.

I realized that I'd seen this bit of river before, in a dozen or so bad nineteenth-century engravings, most of them by untalented but adventurous Germans who had traveled up and down the Mississippi with sketchbooks. The rock on which I sat was exactly where they must have set up their equipment to draw the Falls of St. Anthony. Then the river spilled over a succession of steep limestone steps. It was famously picturesque. The Germans represented the waterfalls by taking a pen and a ruler and making a hatchwork of parallel vertical lines. It must have been a very orderly way of passing an afternoon. They then colored them in with a fierce matte white. The general impression was that at this point the Mississippi was a cascade of toothpaste; one could almost see the army of hired hands squeezing the giant tubes behind the falls. The kindest thing that one could say about the engravings was that they were a vivid illustration of the sheer bewilderment of the European imagination when it tried to confront the raw wilderness of the American West.

For even in the 1800s, this place had been utterly wild—far wilder than the Alps, or the Upper Rhine, or the English Lake District, or any of the other places to which romantic pilgrims went in search of wilderness. Fort Snelling, just downstream, was the last outpost of white America against the Sioux. In 1805, Colonel Zebulon Montgomery Pike led an expedition to the headwaters of the Mississippi and camped beside the Falls of St. Anthony. A Sioux warrior stole the colonel's American flag while Pike was out hunting for geese, swans, ducks, and deer. In his notebook, he was very hard on the local savages and wrote that he had shot "a remarkably large raccoon" on the riverbank.

UNDER PURPLE SKIES

Then the falls had been harnessed to turn mill wheels. The remains of the mills still lined the far shore, their brickwork fallen in, their paddles long gone. They'd ground corn and sawed up forestfuls of timber. The falls had blocked any further navigation of the river to steamboats, and Minneapolis had been the natural place to join the railroad system to the waterway.

In 1861, Anthony Trollope came to Minneapolis by train, but couldn't make up his mind about whether the place, whose name he found delightfully ridiculous, ought to properly be called a village or a town. Mark Twain came here in 1880 and found a city that had swollen to the size of St. Paul, its "Siamese twin." The two cities were the Ronny and Donny of the northwest, joined at the breastbone and the abdomen, facing each other for every second of their lives, interesting to visit, alive, real, and living. By then, sixteen different railroads met up in the desolate sidings at my back, and they were knocking the heart out of the commercial life of the river. In 1904 the Baedeker Guide to the United States, rather at a loss to find nice remarks to make about Minneapolis, was at least able to describe it as "the flour milling capital of the world."

And the river . . . poor, schooled, shriveled river. All this piling up of one technology on top of another—the railroad on the steamboat, the interstate highway on the railroad, the hydroelectric dam on the watermill—had reduced the Mississippi from a wonder of nature to this sluggish canal on the wrong side of the tracks. Bridged, dammed, locked, piered, she was safe now. Minneapolis had no need to bother with her. It had turned its back on the water, and only odd foreigners like me with dreams in their heads came here to brood over what had happened to her.

Out in the stream, the grubby current humped against the giant steel mooring bitts to which no barges were tethered. I thought I saw a dead fish, but it turned out to be a condom. I remembered the old spelling bee, the voices of little girls chanting in a primary-school classroom:

Mrs. M., Mrs. I., Mrs. S.S.I.
Mrs. P., Mrs. P., Mrs. Ippi, Ippi, aye!

The condom went off in pursuit of my cigarette pack—a "French tickler" with a nasty semblance of swimming life. I suppose that some indigent peasant in Yucatán might find use for it when it finally washed up on his beach.

(First published 1981)

156

The Draw of the River: John Berryman

SANDRA SIDMAN LARSON

Washington Avenue Bridge, Minneapolis, Minnesota
January 7, 1972

i
From the bridge in summer,
the university varsity team
can be seen sculling upstream.
Gulls tilt above the river.

Toward winter, fall leaves
ride facedown on the cooling
waters and the gulls are gone,
the water icy.

ii
That winter day, your poems
crowded around you—
some pleading with you
to stay,

some urging you to go.
No poetry left to tell us
what the fall felt like,
what the light was like, or

the letting go.

Mississippi Drift

MATTHEW POWER

I met Matt Bullard on a scorching July afternoon and followed him through leafy, upper-middle-class residential streets toward Minneapolis's West River Park. The industrious hum of weedwackers and leaf blowers filled the air, and helmeted children tricycled along a path, their watchful parents casting a suspicious eye at us. But through a small hole in the foliage by the edge of the bike path, we instantly stepped out of the middle-American idyll, scrambling down a narrow path through the tangled undergrowth, through cleared patches in the woods littered with malt liquor cans and fast food wrappers, hobo camps with the musty wild smell of an animal's den. I clutched at the roots of saplings to keep from tumbling down the slope. The sounds of civilization receded to white noise. We stumbled out of the trees onto a sandy spit, and I suddenly saw the river before me, narrow and amber-colored, flowing silently south, lined on both banks with forested bluffs.

Matt's raft was moored to the bank next to a storm sewer outflow pipe. My first impression was of the Unabomber's cabin set afloat. A brief description of the vessel: ten feet in the beam, twenty-four feet stem to stern, its decks had been laid down over three rows of fifty-five-gallon drums, twenty-three in all. "I got them from a dumpster behind a chemical plant," Matt told me. "Some of them still had stuff sloshing around inside." The barrels had been framed out with lumber, mostly two-by-fours swiped from construction sites, and a deck of marine plywood set on top. On this platform Matt had built a cabin, about ten by fourteen feet, leaving a small motor deck aft and a front porch fore. The porch connected to the cabin through a pair of French doors, and a screen door exited the rear. The cleats, railroad spikes welded to diamond plate, were "punk as fuck," said Matt, admiring his amateur blacksmithing. On the roof was bolted a large solar panel of larcenous provenance, as well as a small sleeping quarters and a worn-out armchair from which the boat could be steered. A wheel salvaged from a sunken houseboat was connected by an ingenious series of pulleys and wires to the outboard motor on the back deck, a thirty-three-horse-power, two-stroke Johnson, which was showroom-new during the Johnson Administration. It was one of the few purchased items on the boat, bought by me as a gesture of my commitment to the mission. Several workbenches lined the cabin, and there was a galley with a propane stove, a chest of drawers, and a rusty high school gym locker for storage. Matt had brought everything he had scrounged that could possibly be of use: old fishing anchors, tied-up lengths of rope, lawn furniture, a folding card table. Three bicycles. Several five-gallon gas tanks. A stereo speaker system, with subwoofers made of paint cans, hooked up to a motorcycle battery. A collection of practice heads from the dumpster of a beauty college. In keeping with the rustic theme, the boat's front had a porch swing made of shipping pallets and a pair of plastic pink flamingos, "liberated from some lawn," screwed to its posts. Matt's six-foot-two frame had bulked up since I'd last seen him, and his hair had grown into a waist-length mullet of dreadlocks hanging behind a battered black baseball cap. He wore a goatee, and his round face squeezed his eyes to mischievous slits when he smiled. He had added to his tattoo collection to form a sort of identity-politics résumé: NOT REALLY VEGAN ANYMORE, advertised an amended dietary philosophy on his wrist; a piece on the back of his hand showed crossed railroad spikes and the free-associative motto, WANDERLUST ADVENTURE TRAMP; on his left bicep was a black-masked figure standing behind a dog, above the phrase, ANIMAL LIBERATION.

Matt hadn't held a steady job since a brief stint at Kinko's in the late nineties. One time in court, he said, a judge had admonished him: "You can't be homeless the rest of your life. You have to work." He laughed as he recalled this. "I fucking hate work," he said. "If I could see some result from it, besides money, maybe I'd do it. I went into the welfare office to apply for food stamps, and they took one look at me and said, 'Clearly, you're unemployable.'" He saw no shame in this, and he looked at food stamps as a way of getting back the taxes he paid when he was at Kinko's. From the hundreds of hours he had put into the boat, it was evident that what he hated was not doing work per se, but rather trading his time for money. Matt had been working on the boat for over a year and had spent almost nothing on it. What wasn't donated or dumpstered was procured by extralegal means. "Half this boat is stolen," he chuckled, with unmistakable pride in his handiwork and resourcefulness.

For Matt, the river trip was to be a sort of last great adventure before he left the United States for good. As long as he stayed, he felt the ultimate unfreedom of jail lurking around every corner. For years he was heavily involved with the animal-liberation movement and logged weeks of jail time in three different states for protests at animal-testing facilities. He claims to be on a domestic-terrorist watch list. "When I get my ID run by the cops, it comes up 'Suspected member of Animal Liberation Front. Do not arrest.'" A recent homecoming for Matt in LAX resulted in a five-hour interview with Homeland Security. He related all these stories with thinly veiled pride, the way a parent might describe a child's performance in a Little League game.

After the river journey, he was moving to Berlin, a squatter's paradise he had visited once and found far more livable than anywhere in the United States. "I hate America," he said, without the menace of a McVeigh or a Zarqawi, but nevertheless with feeling. I asked what he would do with the raft once we reached New Orleans and he left for Germany. "Only one thing to do," he said. "Torch it. I'm gonna give this motherfucker a Viking burial."

***

To inaugurate the voyage, Matt had planned a launch party a mile downstream, at a beach on the river's edge. With a few more arrivals, our little crew swelled to five: me and Matt, plus Cody Dornbusch, a compact, bearded twenty-four-year-old from South Dakota; Chris Broderdorp, a twenty-one-year-old bicyclist and master dumpster-diver from Minneapolis, rail-thin with a half-shaved mop of curls and a high-pitched laugh; and Kristina Brown, a fetching, levelheaded twenty-five-year-old from Seattle, who among them had the most schooling and seemed most to be playacting at the pirate life. I was the only crew member without a pierced septum. The general mood among my boatmates was upbeat: the overflowing dumpsters of Middle America would be more than enough to sustain our bodies, and adventure would nourish our spirits. Matt fired up the ancient engine, and in a haze of blue exhaust smoke we chugged slowly out into the current, which had the color and foaminess of Coca-Cola, and headed downstream, hidden from the city by the limestone bluffs. The abandoned mills around the Falls of Saint Anthony—the falls that had brought the city here—had been converted into million-dollar condominiums. The Minneapolis-St. Paul metroplex, tidy and forward-looking, seemed to have turned its back on the river that birthed it.

The party, advertised among the local punk scene through word of mouth and printed flyers, commenced at sundown. The raft was hung with Christmas lights, and a driftwood bonfire blazed on the sand. Kids drank forties of malt liquor and climbed over and over again onto the roof of the raft, jumping, diving, and cannonballing in various states of undress into the muddy brown river water. The night was humid and sultry, tinged with menace, and a thick darkness pressed down upon the river. Amid all the wild shouting and splashing, the dirt-smudged faces lit up by flames and colored Christmas lights, it seemed as though the raft had run aground on some cargo cult's island, the natives working themselves into a frenzy as they decided whether to worship us or eat us or escort us to the edge of the volcano at spearpoint. Someone stumbled into me in the dark, dripping, and grabbed me by the shirt, smelling of sweat and booze and the river, his voice slurred. "Hey! You're the writer. From New York." I reluctantly confirmed this. "Well, your fuckin' story better be about *solutions*." (He dragged out the word for emphasis.) "Otherwise it's bullshit. Solutions!" His grip tightened. He attempted to fix his gaze to mine and failed. He shouted "Solutions!" once more for good measure before shambling away and jumping into the river again.

In the morning, with the ashes of the bonfire still smoldering and a half-dozen half-dressed casualties of the bacchanal sprawled on the beach, we pulled the lines in and pushed the raft's barrels off the sand bar, drifting out and spinning like a compass needle until the boat nosed at long last into the flow of the river. With the Lyndon Johnson (the nickname I had given the forty-year-old engine) at half-throttle, the raft meandered with the current, the green wall of trees slipping by at walking pace. The five-gallon gas tank was draining disturbingly fast. I sat on the front-porch swing, rereading a dog-eared newspaper. Chris idly strummed a guitar as Cody and Kristina sat up top with Matt, who was steering from the captain's chair. "You know, you're going to be reading that fucking July sixteenth *New York Times* for the next month," Cody told me, sticking his head over the edge. I put the paper down. A Hmong family fished from a railroad embankment, waving excitedly as we passed, perhaps remembering the long-tail boats of their far-off Mekong. Eagles wheeled and dove into the river, which unscrolled before us as we rounded each bend. It was high summer, blue skies and sunny, about as auspicious as one could hope for the start of a two-thousand-mile journey. We had hung up ragged pirate flags, and now they fluttered behind us in the breeze, the grinning skulls wearing a look of bemused delight.

Our first obstacle was Lock and Dam Number One. To maintain a navigable channel on the upper Mississippi, which would otherwise be too low in the summer for commercial traffic, the US Army Corps of Engineers built a system of twenty-nine locks and dams between Minneapolis and St. Louis. These serve as a stairway for ships to survive the Mississippi's 420-foot drop during its 673-mile journey to St. Louis; below that, the river (joined by the Missouri and then the Ohio) is sufficiently deep not to require locks, and there the Corps built levees instead. This engineering work has altered the natural flow of the Mississippi, allowing millions of acres of former flood plains and wetlands to be converted into intensively cultivated industrial farmland, which in turn sends fertilizer- and pollutant-rich runoff from thirty-one states coursing back into the channel and downstream. Floods are held back by levees, and the resulting pressure, like that of a thumb pressed over the nozzle of a hose, erodes 15,000 acres of wetlands a year from the Delta, creating an oxygen-starved "dead zone" the size of New Jersey each summer in the Gulf of Mexico. The Mississippi is one of the most managed, and mismanaged, river systems in the world.

The upper river may be restrained by dams, but it is not without its hazards, both natural and man-made. I flipped through our photocopied set of charts of the upper river, on the cover of which there was a hand-drawn picture of a squarish boat, seen from above as it travels in a circle, about to plow over a stick figure flailing in the water. Underneath was written: CIRCLE OF DEATH. Matt explained this rather gruesome nautical term: when a speedboat operator stands up and catches the throttle, he can be tossed overboard, yanking the tiller to one side. The unmanned boat, at full throttle, will then trace a wide circle and return to the same spot where its pilot was sent overboard, running him down and causing death by hideous propeller wounds. Although the two-mile-an-hour cruising speed of our vessel made such a scenario unlikely, the crew decided to christen our raft the SS Circle of Death.

Each page of the charts covered ten miles of river, and each enumerated a frightening array of obstacles. "Wing dams," long jetties of rocks that jut out into the river to direct flow toward the channel, lurked just inches below the surface, waiting to tear our barrels from under us. "Stump fields," the remnants of clear-cut forest lands that had been drowned by the river, appeared as cross-hatched forbidden zones that would strand us in an enormous watery graveyard. But of the many things we had been warned about, barges were by far the most dangerous. Seventy-five million tons of wheat, soybeans, fertilizer, coal—the bulk produce of mining and industrial agriculture—are shipped by barge along the upper river every year. A standard fifteen-barge tow, three hundred yards in length, can carry the freight equivalent of 870 semi-trucks. They are as large as a high-rise building laid on its side, and about as easy to steer. A tow plying the river under full steam can take as long as a mile and a half to slide to a stop, plowing over anything in its path. The Lyndon Johnson sputtering out in the navigation channel while a tow bore down on us was not something I wished to contemplate.

As if reading my thoughts, just yards from the mouth of the lock chamber, the motor coughed a few times and then quit. We spun in place, and Matt flew down the ladder from the top deck to try to get the engine started. "Shit, shit, shit!" he yelled. "I forgot to mix the oil in with the gas!" The old two-stroke lubricated itself with an oil-gas mix, and we had very nearly blown the engine by running straight gas through it. Matt popped open a bottle of oil and sloshed it into the gas, measuring by eye. The rest of the crew scrambled for our canoe paddles, hacking at the water futilely to try to guide the raft into the lock. Matt barked orders that no one heeded, and the general response of the crew (myself included) to our first emergency was unrestrained panic. Finally, after loud cursing and many wheezing turns of the starter, the engine roared to life, leaving an oily rainbow on the water and a cloud of blue smoke in its wake.

"That's fucking great," said Matt. "Dead fish and dead Iraqis."

The lock loomed ahead of us and we slid into its chamber, cutting the engine and bumping up against the concrete retaining wall. A lock worker walked along the wall to us and threw down ropes to keep the raft in place. I had hoped he'd be excited at our arrival, or at least amused, but he had the world-weary countenance of a man who had seen all things that float, and our jerry-built vessel of scrap lumber and barrels was insufficient to impress him. I asked him what other strange things had passed through his lock. A guy came through rowing a raft of lashed-together logs just last year, he said. I realized that we were just the latest in a long line of fools, and not even the most hard-core.

Behind us, the door to the chamber swung silently shut, and like a rubber duck in a draining bathtub, we began sliding down along the algae-slick wall as millions of gallons of water drained into the next stage of the river. Within a few minutes we had dropped thirty feet, and the top of the chamber glowed distantly as if we were at the bottom of a well. With the majesty of great cathedral doors swinging open, a crack appeared between the gates of the lock, and the murky green waters of the chamber joined the still waters of the lower river, glinting in the sunlight. Matt whooped, to no one in particular. New Orleans, here we come.

Elegy for Bridge 9340,
Minneapolis, 2007

SU HWANG

Steel trusses & gusset plates gave way:
Splintered concrete bones, somersaults

Of beams, barrel vaults & bowstrings.
　　　　Then: Mayhem.
　　　　　　　　Zigzag
　　　　Of cantilevers amid manufactured
Jetties over lock & dam; collapsed

　　　　Bridge. Blare of sirens.
Yellow school bus
　　　　　　Dangling off
The precipice like a suggestion. Pure
　　　　Terror at the height of

　　　　Rush hour: *we interrupt your*
Regularly scheduled programming to bring

You breaking news. Crushed car
　　　　　　Constellations in the murk.

A tractor-trailer on fire. On TV, there's
　　　　Always more horror to assume.

Offscreen: strangers saving strangers
From certain oblivion. I had forgotten

The Mississippi feeds from the North
Woods to the delta—its gnarled

　　　　Tendons stretching
Past cornfields to inland marshes

Where the whisper of tornadoes
Can usher devastation. Doesn't tragedy

Often happen in this fashion—a split
Second decision like having an extra cup

Of coffee or hitting the snooze button?
Coming to a full stop could mean the

Difference between breathing or no longer
Belonging: twist of fate waits for no one,

Not caring where you come from or how
            Much you've saved

For winter. But can we live like this?
Always looking over shoulders as we move

Through channels—across borders? Whether
Manmade or fed by nature, all we can do to

Survive is keep our heads straight on this
Two-way street—remembering to always

                    mind the gap.

Nye's

JULIA KLATT SINGER

We chose Nye's for its piano bar. Mona and I had both been there, but it had been awhile. We had sat in the shiny, glittery gold booths and listened to other people sing. Lou had played the piano there forever, and we were expecting to find her on the bench when we came in that January night. But she was given a couple nights off, and instead it was a round-faced man with thinning blond hair playing away. People bought him drinks and he drank them, fast. He had a boisterous style and when someone wasn't singing, he was all running banter.

We sat in a booth, ordered a beer, and tried to get our nerve up. There were a couple three-ring binders with the words of songs in them that got passed around as Roxy delivered drinks on a tray. A painting of Chopin hung above the piano player's head with a look that said he wasn't all that impressed and maybe resented that this room was named after him. Perhaps resented too, that he had to be there night after night, listening to liquored-up singers marching their way through "Mack the Knife" and "New York, New York."

Not to say there weren't good singers in there—there were. Nancy could belt out a Patsy Cline that made you swoon. And countless other voices filled that room with beauty. But there were also a number of enthusiastic singers who never hit a single note right.

We decided on "King of the Road," because both Mona and I remembered singing it in the car with our dads when we were girls. Mona is my best friend. We'd met in the hallway outside the preschool classroom my son and her daughter were in when they were three. I was very pregnant with my second son, who she's known for his entire life.

There is something to meeting someone in a hallway crowded with small jackets and backpacks large enough for each child to climb in their own. The minutes are precious and stolen, the children darting from hand to leg. Try to have a cup of coffee while the children play with trains under the table. Try to have a conversation while they swing from the monkey bars at the nearby park, always, or almost always, in your peripheral vision.

You find in those moments all sorts of things to laugh about, all sorts of things to consider. That night at Nye's, we decided on "King of the

Road" because we weren't kings of anything, and we both could be nostalgic, both loved the open road, even if we saw it most often in our minds.

It was harder to sing than we imagined. There were verses we didn't know existed and it went on and on and on. We mostly nailed the chorus, but by the third or fourth time we weren't the only ones wishing it over. When we finished, Mike, the piano player said, "Well, you got through that one."

We slinked away from the piano bar, headed as far away from the piano and the singers as we could, and found ourselves standing by a set of swinging doors with small rectangular windows in them. We could hear music coming from the other side. Drums, guitars, a sultry voice singing. On one of the doors was a little black metal sign that said *In*.

It was a bit like falling down the rabbit hole, and I was a bit like Alice. It felt like a world, a fully realized and thriving world. We found ourselves in the middle of a small dance floor, facing the band: a drummer and three guitar players and a woman singing. Three men and one woman were dancing and made space for us to step through.

It was the kind of bar I love. Long and thin, a corner bar, the kind you find in most small towns here in the Midwest. The stage, if you could call it that, that the band was mostly on—two of the guitar players sat in chairs on the dance floor—was no bigger than a closet. There were booths with shiny red Naugahyde against the wall and a bar that ran the length of the place. A jukebox sat at one end of the booths and a photo booth at the other, by the door to the street. We looked for an open stool or two, found them midway down, and bellied up to the bar.

It was crowded enough to be warm, and just open enough to be inviting. We sat down on the stools and waited for the bartender. There was one, a man in his late fifties, working the bar. He moved with a professional ease. His shirt was pressed and spotlessly white and his moustache neatly trimmed.

He stopped, asked us what we'd like. Two Stellas, we told him. We paid in cash and he set our change down in front of us. I looked down at the coins and noticed that one wasn't a coin at all, but a round silver medallion with an angel relief on it. I showed it to Mona, said, "Look at this." When the bartender passed again I showed it to him, telling him, "This is what I got in my change."

"You are something," he said, and offered to swap it for a quarter.

"No," I told him. "I'm taking it, as a sign."

He nodded his head in agreement. This was Mikey. He would become our bartender. He would give us our nickname, the Stella Sisters. He would save us spots at the bar on the nights we are running late by pouring half beers and putting coasters on top of them. He would become the guy Mona sends Christmas cards to every year. We would bring him birthday and holiday presents. We would worry over his health, his heart. I would end up carrying that angel for years in the coin pocket of my jeans.

I would lose it in the sand on a beach on Lake Superior. It would be a hard thing to lose, but I would also realize that it would eventually be lost, like everything that mattered to us about those nights of music and friends. Because nothing lasts forever, even a timeless place like Nye's. I hope someone else finds that silver angel and carries it as long as they can, like I did, as a reminder of who and what matters.

Midnight in the Garden with Claes Oldenburg

TAMI MOHAMED BROWN

I was still young, still new to the city
on that still night off Hennepin
when you wondered:
was the shallow moat meant to distance bodies from structure?

You left your shoes, waded in.
I left all reason to follow you
—not to the ends of the earth—
but to climb the Spoonbridge to the Cherry.

I would have followed you anywhere.

Prince of the Midwest

MICHAEL PERRY

You'd never dream it looking at me all doughy, bald, and crumpling in my fifties, but I owe the sublimated bulk of my aesthetic construct to Prince Rogers Nelson, circa *Purple Rain*. The film and album were released the summer after my fresh-off-the-farm freshman year in college. I sat solo through the movie a minimum of four times, wore the hubs off the soundtrack cassette, draped my bedroom with purple scarves, stocked the dresser top with fat candles, and Scotch-taped fishnet to the drywall above the bed. Intended to create seductive shadows of mystery, it wound up a pointless cobweb.

I furthermore spent time scissoring words and letters out of magazines and taping them around the edges of the bureau mirror to re-create Prince's lyrics in the style of a hostage note, phonetic shorthand included (Prince was text messaging before text messaging). Prior to this, my idea of interior design was a pair of antlers and a linked chain of all my used football mouth guards dating back to seventh grade. But then came Prince.

And my perception of masculinity, of beauty, of my own Midwest, expanded. Expanded a tad more than was sustainable, as it turned out, but expanded. Prince was not my single motivator, but he lit the incense. Within a year of watching *Purple Rain*, I bought my first army surplus trench coat, rode a Greyhound bus out of Wisconsin to work as a cowboy in Wyoming, made my first trip to Europe, and began experimenting with hair mousse.

***

It's tricky, tantamount to tacky, composing postmortem paeans to people of renown. The pitfalls are plenty: reverse-engineered significance, boutique bereavement, the appropriation of grief as virtue-signaling, leveraging fame to which I have no claim.

In fact, I am simply sad that Prince Rogers Nelson is gone.

Hand over heart: I wrote the opening paragraph to this piece the week before he died.

***

For someone growing up in New Auburn, Wisconsin, Minneapolis was the distant mystery city. The few times I ventured across the Minnesota state line, I was a kid riding shotgun in a pickup truck with my dad and a load of lambs, and even then we went only as far as the St. Paul stockyards.

Minneapolis was a skyline cluster, a glow. Once, my grandfather took me to the top of the IDS Center, but he wouldn't spring for tickets to the observation deck. Instead we got a long elevator ride capped by a glimpse of sky. My perception of the metropolis remained that of a sidewalk-level hick craning his neck. I just remember glass and tall.

Then it was back to the farm. Two hours by sheep truck. Northwestern corner of Chippewa County, Wisconsin. Milk the cows, sling the manure, go to church every Sunday. A lean church, with lean beliefs. No movies, no radio, no dancing. Books, though? I had stacks. I was not unhappy.

***

In my memory I recall the scene in *Purple Rain* of Prince and Appolonia making love in the barn. I knew that barn. I knew the light striping through those rough-cut boards. Those rawboned beams. And while my churchly ways and other clumsinesses precluded me ever engaging in anything remotely approaching Prince's gynecological gymnastics, I did indeed know what it was to kiss a girl with chaff in her hair.

All these rural vibes and here's this glittering fellow in stilettos, ridiculous in the context, and yet—down there in the funk—hitting notes that resonated in the heart of a chaste doofus shod in Farm and Fleet clodhoppers. Old Man Johnson's farm? Where Prince took Appolonia on that Hondamatic? Its dead ringer sat right off our back forty. For real. Same barn, same surname. Ed Johnson. You could check the plat.

But coldhearted fact-checking revealed my *Purple Rain* memory to be a conflation over time. The haymow scene wasn't in the film but rather in the trailer. Even then it was just a half-second shot of Appolonia standing in straw. The lovemaking took place elsewhere.

Some of what I recollect was in the "When Doves Cry" video. And Old Man Johnson's farm was name-checked in "Raspberry Beret," which came out the year after *Purple Rain*.

But these little call-outs, these lyric and visual specifics—they threaded my coarse flannel with a strand of purple, connecting the stumblebum to the star.

***

Sometime around 1992, I cowrote a frozen pizza commercial for a company in Eau Claire, Wisconsin. We drove to Minneapolis to edit the video at a production company called Crash+Sues.

By then I'd come to know Minneapolis through a smattering of visits: the Metrodome for a Twins Game, a Neil Diamond concert at the Target Center, a Molly and the Heymakers show at First Avenue, an airport drop-off, a family reunion in the suburbs. In other words, as a tourist. But I knew the way, and the city felt less distant, less mysterious. A Badger State cheesehead to the core, I nonetheless came to think of it as "our" big city. Came a time when Manhattan-based publicists would schedule me on book tour flights out of Milwaukee. "It's a five hour drive to Milwaukee from my farm," I'd say, "But ninety minutes due west of here? Minneapolis! They have an airport there with airplanes that go *all over the world!*"

"But . . . but you live in *Wisconsin!*" They said this more than once.

"Yes," I always replied, "and we have an *open border agreement* with Minnesota."

The Crash+Sues edit suite was set up like a mini-amphitheater. A few rows of desks and seating and the monitors down front. There was no light but the screen-glow. The engineer said Prince had been there to work on a video. Slipped in and sat in the backmost row. Called for cuts and rewinds and playback quietly, but decisively. Then he left. I was taken by this image, of the electrifying performer in economy mode. Doing his work, then departing. Right *here.*

***

I rerun these fragments and uncertain memories not to claim Prince, but rather as thanks for the tangible good he did me. The paragraph I wrote the week before he died was for a chapter on aesthetics in a book about the sixteenth-century French philosopher Montaigne. That is not the sort of tangent a hay bale stacking farm boy follows without felicitous nudges.

I think of my young self trying to be Prince, a foolish pursuit on the face of it, but essential at the heart of it, leading as it did to other gracious worlds. I think of him at work in and around Minneapolis, percolating his purple explosion, and how a few grains drifted across the St. Croix River and settled on my boots.

And if my leaden feet were not lightened, if I did not morph into an irresistible sex machine, I did think, "Well, perhaps I don't have to stay this way." And then, with a lot more clomping than dancing, I found my way into a life beyond the farm, and for the following thirty years went daily to the keyboard, trying to make a little art.

***

We all end up dead meat. I can rhapsodize about the magic of a man even though I know full well he was mortal. But when I looked up from the manuscript I was working on that morning and saw the news, I wasn't prepared for the sense of vacuum. *He was right over there*, I thought, casting my mind across the river. *As early as this morning. Working.*

Working. That was the thing. I never once saw Prince perform live. And even though I'd been to First Avenue—the seminal setting for *Purple Rain*—it took sitting in that little video studio for it to hit me: Minneapolis was where Prince *worked*. And ever since that day, I thought of him in that context. Just across the St. Croix. *Working.*

Thanks to my background—raised by truckers, loggers, and small-patch farmers—I still struggle to get past the dumb trope of sneering at art as work. As if any given roadie hustles any less than any given logger. As if Prince's dance-worn hips would be more honorably won had he ruined them kneeling to milk cows or trowel concrete.

I have an old pickup truck. For plowing snow, hauling firewood, and because no matter how much French philosophy I read, nothing sorts my soul like rolling country roads in that truck. So ten minutes out, when the initial vacuum of the news that he was gone had shifted to soft vertigo, I fetched the truck and drove to my neighbor's place.

This particular neighbor had won some Grammys, and built a recording studio a couple cornfields over. It's not Paisley Park, but it's enough. You can rattle around some if you're alone in there. The only person present was the house engineer, who did a stint with Prince. Some Vegas shows. We sat for maybe five minutes, talking about the artist and his work. The door was open, the spring breeze—still surprising that time of year—riffling lyric sheets on a desk. Prince was demanding, the engineer said. A force of nature. Totally wild and far out, difficult, but 100 percent knew what he wanted. "And if he had more arms and legs and hours in a day," said the engineer, "he would have done it all his own damn self."

***

Right around the 3:55 mark of "The Beautiful Ones," Prince goes to screeching and subsequently tosses off a *Hoo!* that I could never hope to utter, but am utterly able to feel. *Here,* he seems to be saying, *let me articulate that for you.* Then he shoots that shy-sly grin, message being: try to keep up, and you will eat my royal dust.

In a box in my barn there are snapshots of me reporting for skate-guard duty at the roller rink in 1986 wearing pink hair dye and a satin magenta head scarf. Goofy as hell and so short of the mark, but further proof that Prince precipitated profound change.

A friend said Prince created his own creative world around him, something many of us in the Midwest have had to do in one way or another. When I heard Prince, when I saw Prince, I felt moved to be more than I was. The flat-footed white boy lip-syncing "When Doves Cry" in the mirror, knowing full well he couldn't so much as polka in shitkickers, let alone do the splits in high heels, was being propelled down a path toward what the philosopher Montaigne said was the greatest thing in the world: to know how to belong to oneself.

***

The other day I had to explain the Prince symbol to a thirtysomething graphic designer. Time roars on and we soothe ourselves with generalizations and memories. Minneapolis is still a million things I'll never know. But when my book tour is over and the plane descends, I am still a country boy looking for the Metrodome. I can still see Grandpa marveling at the Foshay Tower. I am still riding that sheep hauler home, but in the mirror the skyline glows beneath a thin purple scrim.

I'm Going Back to Minnesota Where Sadness Makes Sense

DANEZ SMITH

O California, don't you know the sun is only a god
if you learn to starve for him? I'm bored with the ocean
I stood at the lip of it, dressed in down, praying for snow
I know, I'm strange, too much light makes me nervous
at least in this land where the trees always bear green.
I know something that doesn't die can't be beautiful.
Have you ever stood on a frozen lake, California?
The sun above you, the snow & stalled sea—a field of mirror
all demanding to be the sun too, everything around you
is light & it's gorgeous & if you stay too long it will kill you
& it's so sad, you know? You're the only warm thing for miles
& the only thing that can't shine.

CONTRIBUTORS

Fathia Absie is a Somali American writer and filmmaker. She is a former Voice of America Journalist and an independent storyteller both in film and on stage. Her first film was *Broken Dreams*, a documentary that explores the collective outcry against the recruitment of the Somali youth in Minnesota by religious fanatics. She hosted the Twin Cities Public Television documentary, *Giving Thanks!* and in 2014, she published a graphic novel, *The Imperceptible Peacemaker*. Absie has appeared in films such as *A Stray* and *First Person Plural*, and is well known for showcasing short stories on Facebook as a motivational means for the Somali people, particularly aimed towards youth. Her latest film, *Pursued*, is about a young Somali American man who is in the pursuit of happiness while being pursued by someone else. She is the founder and curator of the "Eat with Muslims" project which brings Muslims and non-Muslims together over dinner and stories in the hopes of building bridges between communities.

Jason Albert lives in St. Paul. He's written for *Washington Post Magazine*, *Slate*, *Wired*, and others. His stories have also been notable selections in *Best American Essays* and *Best American Sports Writing*.

Adam Regn Arvidson is a landscape architect and writer who has lived in Minneapolis for twenty years and now considers it home. He currently works for the Minneapolis Park and Recreation Board. His essays and design journalism have been featured in numerous magazines and his designs have won local honor awards. He recently published *Wild and Rare: Tracking Endangered Species in the Upper Midwest*, a book about Minnesota's diverse and enthralling landscapes and the species that inhabit them. Follow @adamregn on Twitter and Instagram. A version of "Seasons of Minneapolis," was originally published by the online journal *Numero Cinq*.

Kelly Barnhill lives in Minneapolis with her husband and three children. She is the author of four novels, most recently *The Girl Who Drank the Moon*, winner of the Newbery Medal. *The Witch's Boy* received four starred reviews and was a finalist for the Minnesota Book Awards. Barnhill has been awarded writing fellowships from the Jerome Foundation, the Minnesota State Arts Board, and the McKnight Foundation. Visit her online at kellybarnhill.wordpress.com or on Twitter: @kellybarnhill.

Marge Barrett published a chapbook of poems, *My Memoir Dress*, and a memoir, *Called: The Making and Unmaking of a Nun*. Her work has appeared in numerous journals and anthologies. She has taught in high schools, colleges, and adult programs. Currently, she teaches classes at the Loft Literary Center in Minneapolis and conducts a variety of workshops. She and her husband live in Minneapolis after raising their children in St. Paul.

Julian Bernick was born in Fargo, North Dakota, and came to Minneapolis at the age of nine. A graduate of South High School, he studied at Middlebury College and the Iowa Writer's Workshop before returning to Minneapolis, where he has made his home since 1994. He has published poems in various small press magazines and currently works as a poetry editor for *Whistling Shade Magazine*.

Kris Bigalk is the author of the poetry collections *My Narcissus* (2018, NYQ Books) and *Repeat the Flesh in Numbers* (2012, NYQ Books). Her poems have appeared in *Spillway*, *Paper Nautilus*, and the *Water-Stone Review*. She directs the creative writing program at Normandale Community College and lives in Minnetonka with her three sons.

Todd Boss is a poet, librettist, public artist, and film producer. He is the author of *Yellowrocket*, *Pitch*, and *Tough Luck*. His poems have appeared in *Poetry*, the *London Times*, the *New Yorker*, *NPR*, *Best American Poetry*, and *Virginia Quarterly Review*. He is the founder and Director of the poetry film company, Motionpoems. He teaches at the Loft Literary Center, has served on the board of directors of Ten Thousand Things Theater Company, and has been artist in residence at the Target Studio at the Weisman Art Museum of the University of Minnesota. More at toddbosspoet.com

Jay Botten is a lifelong resident of South Minneapolis. He is a United States Navy veteran, and graduated from the University of Saint Thomas, 1999 (BA Philosophy and Theology), Saint John's University, School of Theology, 2001(MA Theology) and Hamline University, Creative Writing Program, 2017 (MALS). His great-great-grandparents on his mother's side were the first of his family to come here. He has lived most of his life in the Uptown area.

Tami Mohamed Brown received her MFA in creative writing from Hamline University, and is a creative nonfiction editor with *Red Bird Chapbooks*. She has been the recipient of a Loft Mentor Series Award, a Minnestoa Emerging Writer Grant, and an artist residency through the National Park Service. She now lives in Bloomington, Minnesota, with her family but still finds inspiration on her daily bus commute to her office job in downtown Minneapolis. "Midnight in the Garden with Claes Oldenburg" was previously displayed as part of Made Here as poetry on the Block E Marquee in 2013.

Sofia Burford is a dual national (Mexican and American) living in Minnesota, most recently since 2012. She grew up in Mexico, and is a marketing major from ITESM Mexico. She also studied in Paris for a year. She has lived in four different US states (Virginia, Kansas, Florida, and Minnesota) for over fifteen years. She loves to read, and has taken several nonfiction writing courses at the Loft in Minneapolis. She has a loving husband, and three children, whose accomplishments have made her proud.

Joshua Davies was raised in Kenwood. He's written poetry consistently since his teenage years, largely, though not exclusively, in the lyrical mode. He also writes songs and lyrics, primarily blues and roots-oriented American music. This lyric, "Hennepin and Lagoon," is a precursor to a memoir where he's started chronicling not only this rich, deeply influential period in Minneapolis history, but also his own experience growing up with parents embedded in the Dinkytown counterculture and as psychics at the center of the New Age and paranormal community in the Twin Cities from the late 1970s through the early 1990s.

Valérie Déus is a Haitian-American poet and film curator living in Minneapolis. Her work has been featured in the *Brooklyn Rail, Midway, Why Vandalism, Aforementioned Productions*, the *Star Tribune*, the *St. Paul Almanac*, and *BeZine*. Her experimental poetry film short was screened in the second Co-Kisser Poetry-Film Festival in 2012. She is the co-creator of *We/Here*, a neighborhood art journal that highlights local writers and visual artists. When she's not writing, she hosts "Project 35," a local radio show where she plays Haitian music and poetry. She is the programmer of FilmNorth's Cinema Lounge, Minneapolis's longest running film series.

Bill Donahue is a journalist living in New Hampshire. His stories have been published in *Harper's*, the *New Yorker*, the *Atlantic*, and *Outside*. An avid cross-country skier, he has visited Minneapolis for races many times and is in possession of ski waxing secrets that he will never divulge. A version of this story appeared in *National Geographic Adventure*.

Eric Dregni is the author of eighteen books including *Never Trust a Thin Cook, Vikings in the Attic, In Cod We Trust, Midwest Marvels, Follies of Science*, and *Weird Minnesota*. He is a professor of English, journalism and Italian at Concordia University in St. Paul and dean of the Italian Concordia Language Village, *Lago del Bosco,* in the summer, which he wrote about in *You're Sending Me Where?* He lives in Minneapolis with his wife, three kids, and an Australian shepherd named Bacco.

J. D. Fratzke was born in Winona, Minnesota and has been part of the Twin Cities restaurant community since 1992. He is the chef and general manager of Bar Brigade as well as director of culinary operations for Republic Seven Corners, Red River Kitchen, Delicata Pizza, and Gelato and Spring Café at Como Pavillion. He and his kitchen teams are active in promotion and fundraising for many local charitable and activist organizations including Share Our Strength, Save the Boundary Waters, and The Minnesota Animal Humane Society. In 2016 J. D. was presented with the Charlie Award for Outstanding Chef by the greater Minnesota restaurant community, and in 2018 he was selected Best Chef in the Twin Cities by the staff and readers of *City Pages*. He spends his spare time writing, hiking, and kayaking the north country and enjoying life with his wife, Lisa, and daughter Nina Jeann. They live in South Minneapolis. A version of "Homeboy" appeared in the *St. Paul Pioneer Press* under the title, "I was looking for a job, but I found a home."

Shannon Gibney is a writer, educator, activist, a Bush Artist, and a McKnight Writing Fellow. She is the author of *Dream Country*, about more than five generations of an African descended family crisscrossing the Atlantic, and *See No Color*, which won the 2016 Minnesota Book Award in Young Peoples' Literature. Gibney is on the faculty of English at the Minneapolis Community and Technical College, where she teaches critical and creative writing, journalism, and African Diasporic topics. A version of "Minneapolis, Revisited" originally appeared in *Into Quarterly: Volume Three: Minneapolis* (2016).

Dobby Gibson is the author of *Polar*, which won the Alice James Award, *Skirmish* (Graywolf), and *It Becomes You* (Graywolf), which was shortlisted for the Believer Poetry Award. All three books were finalists for the Minnesota Book Award. His full-length collection, *Little Glass Planet*, was published by Graywolf Press in May 2019. His chapbook, *Fickle Sun, Loyal Shadow*, is available from Sixth Finch Books. Born in Minneapolis, Gibson's poetry and essays have appeared in *American Poetry Review*, *Columbia Poetry Review*, *Denver Quarterly*, *Fence*, *jubilat*, the *Iowa Review*, the *New England Review*, *Ploughshares*, and on National Public Radio. He's received fellowships from the Lannan Foundation, the McKnight Foundation, the Jerome Foundation, and the Minnesota State Arts Board. He lives in St. Paul, Minnesota. "The Minneapolis Poem" and "Beauty Supply" were originally published in *It Becomes You* (Graywolf Press, 2013).

Jason Good is the author of three books: *This is Ridiculous. This is Amazing*, *Must Push Buttons*, and most recently a memoir, *Rock, Meet Window*. Despite his traffic concerns, Jason really does enjoy living in Minneapolis. A version of "No, You Turn" appeared in the *Minneapolis Star Tribune* under the title, "Too fast, too slow, too angry: A New Yorker's treatise on Minnesota drivers."

Laurie Hertzel has been the senior editor for books at the *Minneapolis Star Tribune* since 2008. She is the author of a memoir, *News to Me: Adventures of an Accidental Journalist* (University of Minnesota, 2010) and has published articles and short stories in the United States, Finland, and Australia, including in *Brevity*, *Tri-Quarterly*, *South Dakota Review*, *North Dakota Quarterly*, *South Carolina Review*, and elsewhere. She has an MFA in creative nonfiction from Queens University, Charlotte, North Carolina, and teaches at the Loft Literary Center in Minneapolis. She is a board member of the National Book Critics Circle.

Su Hwang is an award-winning (and sometimes, not) poet whose debut poetry collection *Bodega* will be published by Milkweed Editions in 2019. Born in Seoul, she called New York City and San Francisco home before transplanting to the Twin Cities to attend the University of Minnesota, where she received her MFA in poetry. She teaches creative writing with the Minnesota Prison Writing Workshop, helps out at Motionpoems, and is the co-founder of Poetry Asylum, a community-based organization with poet and activist Sun Yung Shin in Minneapolis. Visit her at suhwang.com.

Marlon James was born in Jamaica in 1970. His novel *A Brief History of Seven Killings* won the 2015 Man Booker Prize. It was also a finalist for the National Book Critics Circle Award and won the OCM Bocas Prize for Caribbean Literature for fiction, the Anisfield-Wolf Book Award for fiction, and the Minnesota Book Award. It was also a *New York Times* Notable Book. James is also the author of *The Book of Night Women*, which won the 2010 Dayton Literary Peace Prize and the Minnesota Book Award, and was a finalist for the 2010 National Book Critics Circle Award in fiction and an NAACP Image Award. His first novel, *John Crow's Devil*, was a finalist for the *Los Angeles Times* Book Prize for first fiction and the Commonwealth Writers' Prize, and was a *New York Times* Editors' Choice. James divides his time between Minnesota and New York. "The Revealing Season" was first published in the *Minneapolis Star Tribune*.

Megan Kaplan is a lifestyle writer, editor, and educator based in Minneapolis. Her stories have appeared in *Mpls. St. Paul Magazine*, *Martha Stewart Living*, *Travel + Leisure*, the *New York Times*, and *Town and Country*. She is also the founder of "The Wildling," a spoken word storytelling project for youth.

Neal Karlen is the author of eight books on a range of topics including vaudeville, baseball, religious fundamentalism, and linguistics. He was an associate editor for *Newsweek*, a contributing editor for *Rolling Stone*, and a regular contributor for the *New York Times*. He teaches creative writing at Augsburg College. He wrote the libretto for Prince's rock opera, "3 Chains o' Gold." He is currently writing *Prince Off the Record*, a book about his friendship with Prince. "Prince is Alive! (And Lives in Minneapolis)" is excerpted from "Prince Talks: The Silence Is Broken," published in *Rolling Stone*, September 12, 1985.

Monologist, writer, and playwright **Kevin Kling** graduated from Osseo High School and Gustavus Adolphus College. He has authored five books, *The Dog Says How, Holiday Inn, Big Little Brother, Big Little Mother,* and *On Stage with Kevin Kling*. His book *Come and Get It* was chosen as the 2012 Minnesota Center for Books Arts "Winter Book." His plays have been produced off Broadway, throughout Minnesota, and in regional theaters around the country. He has been awarded fellowships from the National Endowment for the Arts, the McKnight Foundation, the Minnesota State Arts Board, the Bush Foundation, and the Jerome Foundation. He is a

McDowell Fellow and has received the Whiting Award, an NSN Oracle Award, and the A. P. Anderson Award. A frequent contributor to Minnesota Public Radio and Twin Cities Public Television, Kevin was named the Minneapolis Story Laureate by Mayor R. T. Rybak in 2014. "My Brother's Bachelor Party" previously appeared in *The Dog Says How*.

Sandra Sidman Larson, twice nominated for a Pushcart Prize, has four chapbooks to her credit. As a finalist in their 2016 poetry contest, her first full-length book of poetry, *This Distance in My Hands*, was published in March of 2017 by Main Street Rag Press, Charlotte, North Carolina. As a poet perched near the forty-fifth northern parallel, but a wanderer, she is drawn to writing about the landscapes of her imagination and her life, wherever that may take her, from Minneapolis to Antarctica and beyond. Holding an MSW, Sandra managed nonprofit organizations for a career, and as a poet has been writing for thirty years. She is an active member of the Loft Literary Center in Minneapolis and the grandmother of two. A version of "The Draw of the River: John Berryman" was first published in the Twin Cities journal, *Sidwalks*, and later in the anthology *In the Company of Others* (Cup and Spiral Books, Minneapolis, 2017).

Ed Bok Lee is the author of *Whorled* (Coffee House Press), a recipient of the 2012 American Book Award, and the Minnesota Book Award in Poetry, among other works. Lee is the son of North and South Korean refugees and immigrants. Lee grew up in South Korea, North Dakota, and Minnesota, and was educated there and on both US coasts, Russia, South Korea, and Kazakhstan. He teaches literature and writing part-time at Metropolitan State University in St. Paul. "Powderhorn," originally appeared in *Into Quarterly: Volume Three: Minneapolis* (2016), and refers to artist Michael Hoyt's *Rolling Revelry* project (2013), a series of bicycle-and-pedestrian-focused events intent on bringing mobile, publicly projected karaoke to city streets and bike paths.

Doug Mack is the author of *The Not-Quite States of America* and *Europe on Five Wrong Turns a Day*. He has written for the *New York Times*, *Slate*, the *San Francisco Chronicle*, and *Travel + Leisure*. He lives in the Longfellow neighborhood with his family, and has a digital home at www.douglasmack.net.

Steve Marsh is a writer interested in culture, extreme experience, and performance. He's profiled athletes, artists, and leaders in thought and business for *Mpls. St.Paul Magazine*, *New York Magazine*, *GQ*, *Pitchfork* and the *Wall Street Journal*. A version of "The Coldest Game" appeared in *Mpls. St. Paul Magazine* under the title, "The Coldest Vikings Game Ever Played."

Rae Meadows is the author of four novels, most recently *I Will Send Rain*, which was shortlisted for the Langum Prize in American Historical Fiction and longlisted for the International Dublin Literary Award. She is past recipient of the Utah Book Award. She lives with her family in Brooklyn, New York.

David Mura has written two memoirs, *Turning Japanese*, which won the Oakland PEN Josephine Miles Book Award and was a *New York Times* Notable Book, and *Where the Body Meets Memory*. His novel is *Famous Suicides of the Japanese Empire*; his four books of poetry include the National Poetry Contest winner *After We Lost Our Way*, *The Colors of Desire* (Carl Sandburg Literary Award), and *The Last Incantations*. His newest book, *A Stranger's Journey: Race, Identity, and Narrative Craft in Writing*, was published in 2018. He lives in Minneapolis. "Minneapolis Public" originally appeared in his book *Angels for the Burning* (Boa Editions Ltd., 2004).

Luisa Muradyan is originally from the Ukraine and is currently a PhD candidate in poetry at the University of Houston where she is the recipient of an Inprint Jesse H. and Mary Gibbs Jones Fellowship and a College of Liberal Arts and Sciences Dissertation Fellowship. She was the editor in chief of *Gulf Coast: A Journal of Literature and Fine Arts* from 2016-2018. She was also the recipient of the 2017 Prairie Schooner Book Prize and the 2016 Donald Barthelme Prize in Poetry. Her collection *American Radiance* won the Prairie Schooner Book Prize and was published by the University of Nebraska Press. Previous poems have appeared in *Poetry International*, the *Los Angeles Review*, *West Branch*, *Blackbird*, and *Ninth Letter* among others. Her poem "Purple Rain" was originally published by *Rattle*.

Lindsay Nielsen is a Minneapolis-based clinical social worker/psychotherapist, writer, and Paralympian. Lindsay competed in the 2000 Sydney Paralympic games, held multiple world records (400m, 800m, half marathon, marathon), was named 1997 Athlete of the Year by the US Olympic Committee, and at fifty years of age, became the first amputee woman in the world to complete a full Ironman Triathlon. Lindsay has published pieces in *Good Housekeeping*, the *Chicken Soup for the Soul* series, the anthology, *Cup of Comfort for the Grieving Heart*, and the women's anthology, *Showing Up Naked*. She co-wrote a biography of Coach Roy Griak, *Ten Yards Beyond the Finish Line*, has completed a memoir, and is currently working on a book of essays. She has been a clinical social worker/psychotherapist and organizational consultant for over thirty years.

James Norton is the food editor for the *Growler*, a St. Paul-based magazine covering food, drink, and culture. He has written a number of books including *The Master Cheesemakers of Wisconsin*, *Lake Superior Flavors*, and *The Wendigo's Credit Card*.

Robert O'Connell is a writer from Kansas living in Minneapolis. His work has appeared in the *Atlantic*, the *Guardian*, the *New York Times*, and *Deadspin*.

Sheila O'Connor is the author of five novels. Her fiction, poetry, and lyric essays have appeared in *Bellingham Review, Alaska Quarterly Review, Baltimore Review,* and elsewhere. In 2019, her hybrid novel *V* will be published by Rose Metal Press. Her books have been among the Best Books of the Year by Booklist, VOYA, Chicago Public Library, and Barnes and Noble Discover Great New Writers. She teaches in the MFA program at Hamline University and serves as fiction editor for *Water~Stone Review*.

Lars Ostrom lives in Minneapolis. His writing has been published on *McSweeney's Internet Tendency* and in *Mountain Man Dance Moves: The McSweeney's Book of Lists*.

Michael Perry is a *New York Times* bestselling author, humorist, playwright, and radio show host from New Auburn, Wisconsin. Perry's books include *Population 485, Truck: A Love Story, The Jesus Cow,* and *Montaigne in Barn Boots*. He has collaborated on musical projects with Mary Cutrufello, Justin Vernon (Bon Iver), Phil Cook, S. Carey, and the Blind Boys of Alabama. He can be found online at www.sneezingcow.com.

Leif Pettersen (@leifpettersen) is a writer, traveler, PR professional, champion juggler, and author of the history/travel book *Backpacking with Dracula*. He has traveled through fifty-seven countries and lived in Spain, Romania, and Italy.

Bao Phi is a multiple-time Minnesota Grand Slam poetry champ and National Poetry Slam finalist who has been on HBO's *Russell Simmons Presents Def Poetry* and whose work was included in the *Best American Poetry* anthology of 2006. He is the author of *Sông I Sing*, *Thousand Star Hotel*, and *A Different Pond*, which received a Caldecott Honor in 2018. He is currently the program director of the Loft Literary Center. "The Why" is used by permission from *Thousand Star Hotel* (Coffee House Press, 2017), copyright © 2017 by Bao Phi.

Matthew Power (1974-2014) was an award-winning print and radio journalist and a contributing editor at *Harper's Magazine*. His work appeared in *GQ*, *Harper's*, *Men's Journal*, *National Geographic*, and the *New York Times*. His articles were also collected in annual anthologies such as *Best American Travel Writing* and *Best American Spiritual Writing*, and he was a three-time finalist for the Livingston Award for Young Journalists in international reporting. He died in March 2014, while on assignment in Uganda, accompanying British explorer Levison Wood on his attempt to become the first person to walk the length of the Nile. The full version of his story, "Mississippi Drift," was originally published in *Harper's*. Today the Matthew Power Literary Reporting Award supports the work of promising early-career nonfiction writers.

Jonathan Raban is the author of the novels *Surveillance* and *Waxwings*; his nonfiction includes *Passage to Juneau* and *Bad Land*. His honors include the National Book Critics Circle Award, the PEN/West Creative Nonfiction Award, the Pacific Northwest Booksellers' Award, and the Governor's Award of the State of Washington. He lives in Seattle. "The Forgotten River" is excerpted from *Old Glory: A Voyage Down the Mississippi* (William Collins, Sons, 1981) and is used here with the author's permission.

Matt Rasmussen is the author of *Black Aperture*, which won the 2013 Walt Whitman Award, the 2014 Minnesota Book Award for Poetry, and was a finalist for the National Book Award. His poems have been published in the *Literary Review*, *Gulf Coast*, *Water~Stone Review*, *Revolver*, *Paper Darts*, Poets.org, and elsewhere. He received a 2014 Pushcart Prize and was awarded the 2015 Holmes National Poetry Prize from Princeton University. A founding editor of the independent poetry press Birds, LLC, he lives in Robbinsdale, Minnesota. A version of "Elegy for the Metrodome" originally appeared in *Into Quarterly: Volume Three: Minneapolis* (2016).

Marcie Rendon, enrolled member of the White Earth Nation, is a playwright, poet, and freelance writer. She has published four nonfiction children's books; two are *Pow Wow Summer* (Minnesota Historical Press) and *Farmer's Market: Families Working Together* (CarolRhoda). Rendon's debut novel, *Murder on the Red River*, was published by Cinco Puntos Press. Rendon is a community arts activist who supports other native artists/writers/creators to pursue their art. With four published plays, she is the producer and creative mind behind Raving Native Theater, which produced *Bring the Children Home . . .* at the 2015 Minnesota Fringe festival and at three community-based venues in 2015-16. She also co-curated six Raving Native Date Nights in Minneapolis in 2016. In 2016-17 she was a recipient of the Loft's Spoken Word Immersion Fellowship with poet Diego Vazquez. Her poem "Wiigwaasabak" was featured in the St. Paul Almanac's Impressions Project Summer. "Lake Street Teppanyaki Grill and Supreme Buffet" is copyright © 2019 by Marcie Rendon, and used here by permission of the author.

John Rosengren is the author of eight books, including the short story collection *Life is Just a Party: Portrait of a Teenage Partier* (Deaconess), the nonfiction exposé *Blades of Glory: The True Story of a Young Team Bred to Win* (Sourcebooks), and the definitive biography, *Hank Greenberg: The Hero of Heroes* (Penguin). His articles have appeared in more than 100 publications, ranging from the *Atlantic* to *Sports Illustrated*. He has lived in London, Paris, and Florence, but currently resides in his native Minneapolis with his wife Maria and their two children. A version of "Life on an Urban Lake" was originally published in *Lakeshore Living*.

Max Ross's writing has appeared in the *New York Times*, the *Los Angeles Review of Books*, Newyorker.com, *American Short Fiction*, and elsewhere. He grew up in the Bryn Mawr neighborhood and currently lives in San Francisco. "The Secret Handshake" was first published in the *New York Times*'s "Modern Love" column under the title, "A Field Guide to Male Intimacy."

Julia Klatt Singer is the poet in residence at Grace Neighborhood Nursery School and a rostered artist for COMPAS. She is co-author of *Twelve Branches: Stories from St. Paul* (Coffee House Press), and author of three books of poetry: *In the Dreamed of Places* (Naissance Press), *A Tangled Path to Heaven*, and *Untranslatable* (North Star Press). She has co-written two dozen songs with composers Tim Takach and Jocelyn Hagen. Singer's son likes to describe her as a long-haired, sweater-wearing poet and thief.

Danez Smith is a black, queer, poz writer and performer from St. Paul, Minnesota. Danez is the author of *Don't Call Us Dead* (Graywolf Press, 2017), a finalist for National Book Award, and *[insert] boy* (YesYes Books, 2014), winner of the Kate Tufts Discovery Award and the Lambda Literary Award for Gay Poetry. Danez is also the author of two chapbooks, including *black movie* (Button Poetry, 2015), winner of the Button Poetry Prize. They are the recipient of fellowships from the Poetry Foundation, the McKnight Foundation, and a 2017 National Endowment for the Arts Fellow as well as the winner of the inaugural Four Quartets Prize from the Poetry Society of America. Danez's work has been featured widely, including in the *New Yorker*, the *New York Times, Buzzfeed, Best American Poetry*, PBS NewsHour, and on the Late Show with Stephen Colbert. They are a two-time Individual World Poetry Slam finalist, four-time Rustbelt Poetry Slam Champion, and a founding member of the Dark Noise Collective. They co-host the Webby Award nominated podcast *VS* with Franny Choi, sponsored by the Poetry Foundation and Postloudness. Danez is a teaching artist and workshop facilitator nationally and in the Twin Cities. "I'm Going Back to Minnesota Where Sadness Makes Sense" was originally published by the *Michigan Quarterly Review*.

Journalist and author **William Souder** lives near White Bear Lake. He has written several books, including *Under a Wild Sky*, a biography of John James Audubon that was a finalist for the Pulitzer Prize. He is currently at work on a biography of John Steinbeck. A version of "Cycling Season" appeared in the *Minneapolis Star Tribune* under the title "For this Minnesota cyclist, the best days of summer are breezing by."

Sarah Stonich is the author of *These Granite Islands, The Ice Chorus, Fishing With RayAnne* (writing as Ava Finch), and a memoir, *Shelter: Off The Grid In The Mostly Magnetic North*. Her novels *Vacationland* and *Laurentian Divide* are published within the Literary Corridor. More at sarahstonich.com

Francine Marie Tolf's award-winning essays and poems have been published widely in journals such as *Rattle, Spoon River, Water-Stone Review*, and *Contrary Magazine*. She is the author of three full-length poetry collections, most recently *How Still the Riddle* (Pinyon Press, 2017). She has also published a memoir, an essay collection, and a number of chapbooks, including two published by Red Bird Chapbooks of Minnesota. Francine has received grants from the Minnesota State Arts Board, Elizabeth George

Foundation, and Barbara Deming Foundation. She shares an apartment in North East Minneapolis with her golden cat, Lilly.

Gwen Nell Westerman is Dakota, enrolled with the Sisseton Wahpeton Oyate, and a citizen of the Cherokee Nation through her mother. She is the author of *Follow the Blackbirds* (Michigan State University Press, 2013), and the poetry collection *War Mothers Song*. Her work has appeared in *Yellow Medicine Review*, *Water-Stone Review*, *Natural Bridge*, and is included in *New Poets of Native Nations* (Graywolf Press, 2018), where "Dakota Homecoming" first appeared.

Morgan Grayce Willow is working on her fourth poetry collection entitled *Oddly Enough*. Earlier titles include *Dodge and Scramble*, *Between*, *Silk*, and *The Maps are Words*. An award-winning essayist, her prose has appeared in *Water-Stone Review*, *Imagination and Place: Cartography*, *Riding Shotgun*, and the online *BoomerLitMag*. Morgan completed the book arts core certificate at Minnesota Center for Book Arts and exhibited her artist's book *Collage for Mina Loy* in 2016.

James Wright (1927–1980) won the Pulitzer Prize for poetry in 1972 for his *Collected Poems*, published by Wesleyan. His other Wesleyan books include *Saint Judas* (1959), *The Branch Will Not Break* (1963), and *Shall We Gather at the River* (1968). Born in Martins Ferry, Ohio, he enlisted in the US Army in 1946 and participated in the occupation of Japan. He attended Kenyon College and earned his PhD at the University of Washington. His first book, *The Green Wall* (1956), was awarded the Yale Younger Poets Prize. Considered one of the great lyric poets of the twentieth century, Wright's life was tragically cut short by cancer. His son, Franz (1953–2015), was also a Pulitzer Prize-winning poet. They are the only parent and child to win Pulitzers in the same category. "The Minneapolis Poem" is from *Above the River: The Complete Poems*, copyright © 1990 by Annc Wright, published by Wesleyan University Press, and used by permission.

Kao Kalia Yang is a Hmong-American writer. She is the author of *The Latehomecomer: A Hmong Family Memoir* (Coffee House Press, 2008), winner of the 2009 Minnesota Book Awards in Creative Nonfiction/ Memoir and Readers Choice, and a finalist for the PEN USA Award in Creative Nonfiction and the Asian Literary Award in Nonfiction. Her second book, *The Song Poet* (Metropolitan Books, 2016) won the 2016

Minnesota Book Award in Creative Nonfiction Memoir. It was a finalist for the National Book Critics Circle Award, the Chautauqua Prize, a PEN USA Award in Nonfiction, and the Dayton's Literary Peace Prize. Yang is also a teacher and a public speaker.

Raised in a nomadic upbringing, **Ahmed Ismail Yusuf** is the author of three books: *Gorgorkii Yimi*, a collection of short stories in Somali, *Somalis in Minnesota*, and *The Lion's Binding Oath*, a collection of short stories. His short stories have appeared in *Bildhaan: International Journal of Somali Studies* and *Mizna: Arab-American Literary Magazine*. His play *A Crack in the Sky* was produced by the History Theatre in St. Paul in February 2018. Other publications have appeared in *Journal of Muslim Mental Health*, *Social Psychiatry* and *Psychiatric Epidemiology*, the *International Society for Traumatic-Stress Studies*, and *Psychiatry Times*. Ahmed has a BS in creative writing and psychology from Trinity College in Hartford, Connecticut, and an MPA (Master of Public Affairs) from the Humphrey Institute of Public Affairs of the University of Minnesota.

Peggy "Pearl" Zambory is a long-time resident of Northeast Minneapolis and the author of "Pearl, Why You Little . . ." a blog she wrote daily for eight years, where a version of "The Party Bus" originally appeared under the title "Minneapolis, Late Saturday Night." You can find it here: http://pearl-whyyoulittle.blogspot.com. Peggy's hobbies include listening in, slowly working herself to death, and bubble baths. She has one cat (Dolly Gee Squeakers, formerly of the Humane Society Squeakers) and commutes daily via the MTC.

ABOUT THE EDITOR

Frank Bures is a writer raised in greater Minnesota and based in Minneapolis. He is the author of *The Geography of Madness* and the editor of the *Lester Literary Update*. His work has been included in the *Best American Travel Writing* anthologies and won other awards. More at frankbures.com.

ACKNOWLEDGEMENTS

The first and biggest thanks goes to you, the reader. Without you there would be no books, no bookstores, no essays, no poems, no writers. So thank you for making it possible for us to write about this place, and for our writings to be collected here.

Next, a huge thanks to the writers in this anthology, many of whom the editor personally browbeat and/or guilted (Norwegian roots) into lending their valuable time and talent to this project for a dubious return. The fact that most of them didn't take much, if any, convincing, and many even offered to write original pieces, indicates how much they care for the contours of our literary landscape.

To the Loft Literary Center, which does so much to foster our literary community, we owe a deep debt. Now with the WordPlay Book Festival, that debt runs even deeper. Thank you for making this a great place for writers to live, work, learn, and teach.

Thank you booksellers. We love you, and we know that you champion our writers whenever you can. May your coffers run over with sales of *Under Purple Skies*.

Thanks to Anne Trubek at Belt Publishing for bringing this collection into being, and for giving cities across the Midwest a voice through Belt's City Anthology series. I hope they are all as much of a joy to curate as *Under Purple Skies* was.

Thanks to Laurie Hertzel for writing the lovely introduction she contributed, and for delving into her family's literary history. But even more so, thank you, Laurie, for the work you do editing the "Books" section of the *Minneapolis Star Tribune*, where you strive to showcase local writers, publishers, and literary events, and to provide a virtual town square for us bookworms.

A special thanks to Jason Albert, a great writer and friend (by way of Wisconsin, but no one's perfect), who volunteered to help with this project as soon as he heard about it, with no expectation of pay or recognition. He would probably rather not be mentioned here, but the fact is he did much of the grunt work, helped edit and give insightful feedback throughout, and played a key role in bringing this collection to life. (He also contributed what I think is one of his best essays for the collection.)

Lastly, thanks to all of you who participated in our fund drive to pay our writers something closer to what they deserve. You've helped shape the stories we'll be reading and telling in the Twin Cities for years to come: Laura Aase, Richard Albert, Suzanne Asher, Patti Baker, Frank and Ruth Bures, Michelle Bellanger, Jonathan Carnes, Martha Clarkson, Alex Cole, Todd Demerath, Michael Dickel, Angela Dornbusch, Katharina Eggers, Robert Esler, Mary Flynn, Heather Fokken, Arthur Gandy, Tom Grant, Mara Hvistendahl, Molly Johnson, Jeffrey Johnson, John Jordan, Elaine Klaassen, Stephanie Koehler, Dora Kripapuri, Amber Lampron, Sandra Larson, Song Lee, Jennifer Linde, Robert Malcomson, Annie Mason, Meleah Maynard, Eileen McIsaac, Tim Murphy, Preston Olson, Steph Opitz, Scott Parker, Lauren Reichel, Grace Riley, John Serio, Ashley Shelby, Emily Sohn, Amber Stoner, J. Ryan Stradal, Bryan Thompson, Berit Thorkelson, Mandy Weilandt, Gwen Westerman and Marianne Zerbe.